D0518359

WORLD WAR I

WORLD WAR I

AMERICA AT WAR

★ ★ ★ ★ ★

Peter I. Bosco
John Bowman, General Editor

Facts On File

WORLD WAR I

Facts On File, Inc.
460 Park Avenue
New York, NY 10016
USA

Library of Congress Cataloging-in-Publication Data

Bosco, Peter I.
    World War One / Peter I. Bosco.
        p.   cm.—(America at war series)
    Includes bibliographical references and index.
    Summary: Tells why America abandoned its isolationism to participate in World War I, and its significance for America.
    ISBN 0-8160-2460-X
    1. World War, 1914–1918—United States—Juvenile literature.
    [1. World War, 1914–1918—United States.] I. Title. II. Series.
D570.A1B67 1990
940.3'73—dc20   90-49086

A British CIP catalogue record for this book is available from the British Library.

Facts On File books are available at special discounts when purchased in bulk quantities for businesses, associations, institutions or sales promotions. Please contact our Special Sales Department in New York at 212/683-2244 (dial 800/322-8755 except in NY, AK, or HI) or in Oxford at 865/728399.

Series interior and jacket design by Ron Monteleone
Composition by Facts On File, Inc.
Manufactured by the Maple-Vail Book Manufacturing Group
Printed in the United States of America

10 9 8 7 6 5 4 3 2

This book is printed on acid-free paper.

CONTENTS

To all the people who inspired and nurtured my love of history when I was in my teens, especially my three high school social studies teachers, Robert Carr, Al Ainbinder and David Rood, and the late historian Barbara W. Tuchman.

FOREWORD

World War I is the name given to the fire that consumed Europe from 1914 to 1918. Before it was over, the flames would spread to six continents.

Mighty nations locked themselves into a titanic struggle. As the months and years passed, it was called simply the Great War—the only description that seemed appropriate. Not until the outbreak of a second struggle in 1939 was the "Great War" recognized as the first of two world wars.

World War I destroyed people, resources and empires. It rocked the political balance of Europe, interrupted its economic growth and decimated a generation of its youth. It started the disintegration of the colonial system that seemed so permanent in 1914. It also released communism as a world force.

The war brought about spectacular shifts of power. Most notable was the rise of the United States to military and economic leadership. As the war reduced the great powers of Europe to a state of impotency, it thrust the United States, unprepared, into a position of world responsibility.

This is the story of that terrifying conflict, and the important role that America played in it.

WORLD WAR I

☆ 1 ☆

THE SINKING OF THE "LUSITANIA"

Fog enveloped the British ship *Lusitania* the entire morning of Friday, May 7, 1915. Captain William Thomas Turner felt greatly relieved when the blinding mist lifted shortly before noon. He was guiding his ship through troubled waters that morning. His grand vessel, a luxury ship of the Cunard line, was carrying 1,257 passengers—159 of them Americans and 168 infants and children.

The ship was on course to her destination, Liverpool, England. Now, as she approached the coast of Ireland, the liner entered waters that were known to be infested with torpedo-laden German submarines, called U-boats (from the German for submarine, *Unterseeboot*). Captain Turner felt uneasy.

Great Britain was at war with Germany, which had issued orders to interrupt all British trade. The plan was to prevent any supplies, from food to arms, from getting to the enemy. Every ship was suspect. Even passenger liners, which would make a good cover-up and might secretly be carrying much-needed supplies.

The fog had made some of the passengers and many of the 702 crewmen on the ship nervous. Many of them had listened to the photographers and reporters at Pier 54 in New York on Saturday, as the ship was being prepared to begin her journey. These journalists had claimed this would be the "Last Voyage of the *Lusitania*."

By early afternoon, the mood had changed to near giddy confidence. The fog cleared away, the day got bright and the ship was close enough to land for the captain and passengers to see the Irish coastline, with its trees, rooftops and church steeples. Some people went to the dining room to eat lunch, expressing to each other their relief at having crossed the Atlantic safely. Others went to their rooms to pack their bags, anticipating their arrival in Liverpool early the next morning.

On deck, 63-year-old Captain Turner felt uneasy. The Irish Coast Patrol, charged with protecting ships in this area, was not in sight. The *Lusitania* remained alone on the flat, blue-green water. Why were there no other ships? he wondered.

To add to the captain's worries, his wireless operator had received several messages the evening before from the British Admiralty, cryptic telegraphs that warned of "Submarines active off south coast of Ireland." This was precisely where his ship now cruised. Captain Turner would have been even more nervous had he known that in the past week 23 merchant vessels had been torpedoed in the waters where he was now travelling.

He tried to dismiss his fears, gazing at his vessel, which had made 201 successful trips since her launching in 1907. The 790-foot *Lusitania* was big enough to carry a flotilla of U-boats on her deck, he reasoned; the bridge was as high as a six-story building. She was fast, with a top speed of 25 knots. That gave her a considerable margin over the fastest U-boats.

The captain smiled wryly as he remembered being questioned by a reporter about the U-boat threat six days earlier, just before sailing. Breaking into laughter, he had responded "Do you think all these people would be booking passage on board the *Lusitania* if they thought she could be caught by a German submarine? Why, it's the best joke I've heard in many days, this talk of torpedoing!"

Captain Turner quickly brought his thoughts back to the present, shaking his head in disbelief that not a single escort ship was in sight. One thing became clear to him. On his present course, at full speed, he would arrive at Liverpool far ahead of full tide. That could mean dangerous circling in these unsafe waters for several hours. He had no choice. He had to change course and backtrack. At 1:45 P.M. the helmsman, on the captain's reluctant orders, swung the *Lusitania* away from the coast.

Some passengers had come on deck by this time, having finished lunch. With heavy hearts, they watched the friendly, green land disappear.

Within 10 minutes, it was the *Lusitania* that was being watched. Kapitänleutnant Walther Schwieger, the 32-year-old skipper of the *U-20* a 650-ton U-boat stationed in the coastal waters of the British Isles, had picked up something in his binoculars. It was a rapidly materializing speck coming in from the west that the skipper noted in his log to be "a large passenger steamer."

THE BRITISH PASSENGER LINER "LUSITANIA," LAUNCHED
IN 1907, DOCKS FOR THE FIRST TIME IN NEW YORK.
(LIBRARY OF CONGRESS)

The 35 men and three other officers on the U-boat came immediately alive as they heard the skipper's command, "Diving stations."

This was Commander Schwieger's first patrol aboard a U-boat in the nine-month-old war. His mission was clear. Any ship believed to be carrying cargo that would aid the enemy must be sunk. Since even food supplies came under that category, all ships were in jeopardy. The *Lusitania*, in fact, was carrying 4,200 cases of small-caliber cartridges and other munitions.

On the *U-20*, Commander Schwieger prepared himself for the command that would send one of his boat's torpedoes—packed with 290 pounds of a powerful new explosive—zooming toward the enemy ship. He stood, his eye tight against the periscope. At 2:09 P.M. came the shout

"Torpedo ready!" A moment later, Commander Schwieger ordered "Fire!" He heard the hiss of air in the foreward torpedo room. The whole sub shuddered from the release of its deadly projectile.

Captain Turner was looking back at the barely visible Irish coastline, as he stood on the port side of the lower bridge. Then he heard the message shouted through a megaphone on the starboard side. One of his seamen had suddenly seen a telltale white streak in the water, coming straight-arrow toward the ship. "Torpedo coming on the starboard," he screamed into the megaphone.

As the captain looked up, the torpedo was so close he could see the foam it raised just before it hit. A deafening explosion was followed shortly after by a second explosion. The ship immediately began to list badly to one side, while plunging ahead erratically. The coast was again in sight. Captain Turner, in the first few minutes after impact, believed he could get the ship to shore, if she could only stay afloat another hour.

That never happened. The captain and his remaining crew could not "right" the ship. It took only 18 minutes to sink the incredible ship that, like the *Titanic*, had been called unsinkable.

It was 18 minutes of tragedy. Dozens of seamen skilled in lifeboat launching and handling were killed below by the first impact of the torpedo. Those remaining, and some of the passengers, tried to release lifeboats.

A debacle followed, as the lifeboats, cut loose on a moving ship that was tipping on her side, swung out and back. The boats crashed against the ship, spilling the people who had climbed into them and then falling on the passengers as they floundered in the water. Of the 48 lifeboats, only six made it to sea, intact with survivors.

Some of the passengers and crew found ways to save themselves in the cold waters by hanging on to pieces of wood or some other material that floated. Captain Turner stayed with his ship to the bitter end. Once in the sea, he saved himself by hanging on to a chair. Eventually, rescue boats reached the few, badly shaken survivors.

When the final count came in, the tally was grim—1,201 dead. Of the 129 children, 94 were gone; of the 35 infants on board, 31 had died; of the 159 Americans, 124 had perished.

To understand how such an event could have happened in a civilized world calls for a close look at the war then in progress. Only then can one realize the scope of this tragedy, and what effect it would have on the United States.

✯ 2 ✯

STORM CLOUDS OVER EUROPE

KAISER WILHELM II
(LIBRARY OF CONGRESS)

The First World War was about nine months old when the *Lusitania* became one of its countless victims. The origins of the war, however, went back to the 1800s.

The nations of Europe changed immensely in the second half of the 19th century. Improvements in health care and nutrition prompted a population boom. The Industrial Revolution was making the European nations more powerful than ever before. The need for new markets and raw materials to keep their factories busy spurred competition among the growing empires for new territory and for influence among smaller nations.

This competition inevitably led to friction. As the British, French and German empires carved up Asia and Africa, heated disputes arose over colonial boundaries. In eastern Europe the disputes between the Austro-Hungarian and Russian empires were even more heated as they vied for control and influence over the little countries of southeastern Europe.

It was Germany that grew most spectacularly. Germany soon became the dominant political power of continental Europe, as well as the strongest industrial and military power on Earth.

Germany's military machine had won a shocking string of victories culminating with the defeat of France in 1871. Frenchmen could never forget the sight of German soldiers in their menacing spiked helmets marching in triumph through the streets of Paris. As part of the price France had to pay for losing the war, Germany added to its empire a whole French province and most of another. This conquered territory, called Alsace-Lorraine, remained a constant thorn to French pride.

From the 1890s onward, Germany's emperor, Kaiser Wilhelm II, symbolized his country's militaristic character. Wilhelm was a tense and immature man who was known for his frequent temper tantrums. His sinister black moustache jutted upward in spikes from under his sharp nose. He always stood straight and rigid. (No doubt he held himself all the more erect to make up for his left arm, withered since birth, which hung uselessly at his side.) He almost always wore a military uniform.

The kaiser's bristling moustache, stiff posture and gaudy, medal-bedecked uniform was made familiar throughout the world by foreign cartoonists, who used him as a convenient symbol of Germany. Throughout his reign, he was preoccupied with enlarging Germany's combat forces. He delighted in flaunting his army and navy.

The intensity of Germany's military buildup worried the other countries of Europe. The French feared another German invasion. The Russians were disturbed by the kaiser's growing friendship with Russia's rival, Austria-Hungary. The British were extremely unsettled by the expansion of the German navy, which might one day be used to challenge Britain's traditional rule of the seas.

As suspicions festered, each nation increased its armed forces to keep pace with its neighbors. As a result of this arms race, armies grew tremendously in size and strength. The generals believed victory would go to the army that was strongest when war broke out.

Politicians tried to arrange a "balance of power" by forming alliances between countries. They hoped that if no group became stronger than the others, peace could be maintained.

Yet, rather than prevent war, the alliance system seemed to increase the risk of a conflict. If a nation felt itself threatened, it might decide to attack first. Allies, bound by agreement, might then be drawn in. A widespread conflict might result, even if none of the countries concerned really wanted it to happen.

The summer of 1914 was a particularly lovely one in Europe. In the fertile fields cows fattened and crops ripened under the warm sun. In the cities commerce flourished and business boomed. Europeans basked in prosperity and peace.

But a terrible storm was looming on the horizon. By this time, two powerful, opposed military alliances had formed: Germany and Austria-Hungary (the so-called Central Powers) on one side, and France, Britain and Russia (later known as the Allies) on the other. Europe had become a huge, armed camp, divided against itself.

It was an extremely dangerous situation, based on mutual distrust, suspicion, rivalry and fear. It was a keg of gunpowder waiting to explode. Only a spark was needed for a massive, all-destructive war to erupt.

An assassin's bullet was to be the spark. For some time trouble had been brewing between Austria-Hungary and Serbia, a small country on its southern border. The Serbs, like the Russians, belonged to the Slavic race. In the Austro-Hungarian provinces that bordered Serbia lived several Slavic peoples, including Serbs, called South Slavs, or Yugo-slavs. With the spread of nationalism these people came to think of themselves as one. Neighboring Serbia pledged to free all Yugoslavs from the control of the Austro-Hungarian empire.

On June 28, 1914, the heir to Austria-Hungary's throne. Archduke Franz Ferdinand was assassinated by a Slav nationalist. The murder was linked to Serbia. After a bitter month of confrontation and tension, Austria-Hungary declared war on Serbia on July 28. Kaiser Wilhelm gave the Austrians his pledge of support.

Russia rose to Serbia's defense and began to assemble troops on Austria-Hungary's eastern frontier. Germany demanded that Russia withdraw its army. Not receiving a reply to this demand, Germany declared war on Russia on August 1. France and Britain honored their agreement to stand by their ally, Russia. Within three days they too were at war with the Central Powers.

World War I had begun.

✳ 3 ✳

THE OPENING CLASH

"You'll be home before the leaves have fallen from the trees," Kaiser Wilhelm told his troops departing for the front. Both sides, in fact, expected it to be a short war. German, French and Russian military planners assured their governments that their enormous forces would need only a few months to vanquish the enemy.

Even before the official declarations of war, the involved countries began to assemble armies on their frontiers. For the huge armies of 1914, this process, called mobilization, was a complex operation.

The monumental task of pulling together millions of men and thousands of tons of equipment and supplies would not have been possible without the recent expansion of the European railway system. Large units of men could be concentrated or shifted around very quickly by railroad. Once away from the railroad stations the armies could move no faster than those of Caesar or Napoleon.

For this reason, control of key rail centers was a central feature of military planning throughout the war. The railroads also helped give World War I a dimension previously unthinkable. For example, in 16 days (August 2 through 18) France transported 3,781,000 persons under military orders, in 7,000 trains.

The German army was the best fighting force in the world. Its soldiers had a high level of both fitness and vigorous training. It also had more heavy artillery than all the Allied countries combined.

The Austrian army was, in general, of poor quality for a major country. Troops lacked adequate training. Also, it was an army drawn from more than a dozen different ethnic groups. Most of its officers could not speak the same language as their men.

France's army was second only to Germany's. The French army had a long and proud history. Her soldiers were full of dash and courage. However, because of France's much smaller population, her potential military manpower was only 60% of Germany's.

Russia mobilized the largest army that had ever existed. This Russian army, however, was not well prepared for war. It had crippling shortages of equipment, ammunition and other necessary supplies. There would be times when many soldiers had to march into battle without rifles.

Britain's army was much smaller than those of the other powers. The British had always relied on their navy, the largest in the world, for protection. Britain was the only nation in Europe that did not have compulsory military service. In August 1914, it had only about 100,000 men available to fight in France. Though small in numbers, these men, called the British Expeditionary Force (BEF), were probably the best trained professional soldiers in the world.

As the Earth's mightiest armies were preparing to annihilate each other, Americans all across the United States followed the events in Europe with keen interest. American newspapers faithfully reported every detail of the crisis. The declarations of war in August 1914 were the biggest news story of the young century.

Some of the fascination with Europe's troubles stemmed from the close connection between the American people and Europe. One out of every nine people living in America had been born in Europe. Six million came from central and eastern Europe, 4.2 million from northwestern Europe and 1.5 million from southern Europe. In addition, more than 18 million native-born Americans had foreign-born parents.

The U.S. government for a time feared that the warring countries would try to stir up trouble in the U.S.A. by appealing to the loyalties of their former subjects. But most foreign-born Americans had come to the United States to escape what they felt were petty squabbles of corrupt and greedy Old World states.

As Europe plunged into war in the first weeks of August 1914, the United States declared that it would not interfere. The majority of American citizens supported the government's policy of neutrality. While the situation in Europe was making headlines, most Americans were content to just read about it.

The fighting began on August 4. On that day the Germans invaded the neutral country of Belgium. Germany had no quarrel with Belgium. Yet German military strategists had long planned the invasion. The reason was that they wanted to use Belgian territory as a sort of "shortcut" to Paris by outflanking the main French forces farther south.

Germany did not want to go to war with Belgium, but Germany's generals needed that country's flat, open landscape and fine rail network to maneuver its tremendous army against France. The kaiser made several pleas to Albert, king of the Belgians, to let German forces pass peacefully through his nation to the French border.

Albert refused. The proud king would not allow German soldiers to trample through his little country without a fight. Although Belgium's small army was no match for its gigantic opponent, the Belgians fought on harder and longer than anyone expected. King Albert's soldiers made a brave and gallant effort to hold back the invaders. Germany's superior arms and greater numbers finally overwhelmed them.

On August 20 the German army entered Brussels, Belgium's capital. Albert and his army eventually retreated to the westernmost tip of his country. They refused to surrender and held out there for the rest of the war. The Germans would try, but never succeeded, in dislodging Albert and his men from that last, tiny patch of Belgian soil.

Americans were shocked by the invasion. Germany's violation of a harmless, neutral country seemed uncivilized. Far worse was the barbaric behavior of German soldiers. Soon after they marched into Belgium, accounts of German atrocities began to appear in American newspapers.

The German army ravaged and plundered the countryside as it advanced. Soldiers tried to terrorize townspeople by randomly taking hostages. They executed about 5,000 hostages, including many Catholic priests. In addition to murdering civilians, the Germans destroyed many buildings and historic landmarks.

One of Belgium's most cherished national treasures was the medieval library in Louvain, founded in 1426. It contained many priceless, ancient manuscripts. German troops burned it to the ground, and much of the city as well.

On August 28, three days after the sacking began, Hugh Gibson, a diplomat from the American embassy in Brussels, came to see Louvain for himself. The city was still burning. Black smoke and soot were everywhere. Even where the flames were gone, the pavement was still hot. The bloated bodies of dead civilians and dead horses lay strewn about.

German soldiers were going street by street, house by house, breaking down the doors and kicking out the people living there. In each house these soldiers first stuffed their pockets with whatever valuables they found there, then set fire to the house. One German officer in charge of this systematic looting and destruction said to Gibson: "We will teach

GERMAN SOLDIERS ATTEMPT TO DEFEND THEIR EXPOSED
POSITION AGAINST FRENCH ATTACK, SOMEWHERE ON THE
WESTERN FRONT IN 1914. NEW RAPID-FIRE WEAPONS MADE THIS
KIND OF DEFENSE OBSOLETE AND LED TO TRENCH WARFARE.
(NATIONAL ARCHIVES)

[the Belgians] to respect Germany . . . People will come here to see what we have done!"

Such reports horrified the American people. Newspapers across the United States condemned the savagery of the Germans. The brave Belgians, who had stood up against the big German bully, were hailed as heroes. Cartoons showed Kaiser Wilhelm as a sinister, overbearing brute trying to stretch his greedy hands, stained with Belgium's blood, across the European continent.

President Woodrow Wilson urged his countrymen not to take sides. "Be impartial in your thoughts as well as action," he said. Yet he was, himself, deeply disturbed by Germany's actions.

Britain and France belatedly sent troops to help defend Belgium. They could not hold their ground against the German "bulldozer." On August 22, the French were defeated at Charleroi (Belgium) and forced to retreat. The Germans attacked the British the next day at Mons (Belgium). The British Expeditionary Force fought well and honorably, but was also forced to retreat.

By August 25 a million German soldiers had crammed into Belgium, poised to pounce on Paris. They swept into northern France, toward the French capital, crushing all resistance.

Meanwhile, in the east, the Russian army was marching into German territory. The early success of this invasion raised the hopes of the Allies fighting in France. Then the Russians suffered a disastrous defeat at the battle of Tannenberg (August 25–31). A large part of the Russian force disintegrated, losing about 125,000 men, the majority taken prisoner. Russia never completely recovered from this catastrophe.

Ironically, the only Allied army not defeated in that first month was Serbia's. Austria-Hungary's invasion of her little neighbor was a fiasco. By the end of August the Austrian army had lost a humiliating 40,000 men and was hurled off Serbian soil.

The first days of September were dark, desperate hours for the Allied armies fighting in France. One German unit came within 15 miles of

GERMAN MACHINE GUNNERS FACE RUSSIAN TROOPS
ON THE EASTERN FRONT, 1915.
(NATIONAL ARCHIVES)

Paris. The exhausted German troops, however, had been pushed to their limit by their commanders and stopped along the Marne River northeast of Paris.

The Allies counterattacked. The battle of the Marne (September 6–10) stopped the Germans in their tracks and forced them to pull back and reorganize their position. The threat to Paris dissolved, along with the kaiser's hope for a quick, victorious war.

The Allied armies were too weak and tired to chase the Germans as they withdrew from the battle of the Marne. This gave the Germans time to dig in.

The early weeks of autumn saw many vicious clashes as both sides tried to hold on to as much ground as possible. The Germans' attempt to push the Allies off the last little piece of Belgium resulted in the first battle of Ypres (October 17–November 21). Casualties were staggering on both sides. The British Expeditionary Force was practically wiped out, but the Allied line held.

By December 1914, trench warfare—the horrible deadlock that characterized the First World War—had arrived. Both sides carved a line of fortified trenches across the face of Western Europe. It was a scar that stretched more than 400 miles from the Swiss border to the North Sea coast. Along these lines millions of men and thousands of artillery pieces were put into position.

The proud armies that marched to war in August were all but gone. Their best soldiers were killed, mutilated and maimed. Each nation had to recruit more men into its army to replace the losses. Many volunteered, but most were drafted. Younger, inexperienced, less well-trained men had to be sent to fill the ranks.

On Christmas Day 1914, both sides declared a 24-hour armistice, or cease-fire. For the freezing troops huddled in their damp dugouts eating canned food, it wasn't much of a holiday. At least there was no shelling from enemy guns.

On December 26 the shooting and shelling resumed. It was if the exasperated armies had paused for a moment to take one last, deep breath before continuing a struggle that would stretch on for years.

Europe in 1915

The Allies	The Central Powers	Neutral nations

⋆ 4 ⋆

THE GREAT NEUTRAL

"THE GREAT NEUTRAL" SET TO MUSIC—1914.
(SMITHSONIAN INSTITUTION)

The year 1915 arrived to find Europeans still shooting at each other, and Americans still distant from the war and wanting to keep it that way. America had always tried to steer clear of Old World conflicts. The United States had embraced a policy of isolationism since the earliest days of the Republic.

The president, peace-loving Woodrow Wilson, concentrated his efforts on domestic programs and issues. Following George Washington's advice, he vowed not to involve the nation in "foreign entanglements."

Yet America had changed a lot since Washington's day. At the time of the Revolution there were three million people in the United States. In 1915 the population reached 100 million, larger than any European country, save Russia. Washington's America of the 18th century was a rural society based on small farms. Wilson's America of the 20th century had become a great industrial power.

America's global trade had rapidly expanded. The U.S. economy was increasingly interwined with Europe's. The days of America's isolationism were numbered.

The most immediate effect of the war on the United States was the disruption of international trade. The Allies and the Central Powers obviously stopped trading with each other. The Allies also wanted neutral countries to stop trading with Germany.

Neutrals had a legal right to conduct business with whomever they liked. The United States, the wealthiest and most important neutral, insisted that the Allies respect that right. Yet the Allies were determined to get their way.

Britain, with her fleet, attempted to starve out the enemy by blocking off all German ports. That blockade was probably the most effective and devastating use of naval power of the war. In this way the Allies cut the Central Powers' outside sources of supply. The gigantic amounts of food and raw materials essential to sustaining a prolonged war would have to be found at home or come from neutral states that could be reached by land.

The United States resented Britain's high-handed tactics. Preventing neutral countries from trading with the Central Powers was a violation of international law. American ships were being stopped, boarded and searched. Even cargoes of grain or beans were considered contraband and confiscated. President Wilson became furious with Britain.

The situation paralleled a crisis 102 years earlier when the British navy blockaded the ports of Napoleon's French Empire, and boarded American merchant ships. That, of course, resulted in the War of 1812.

In 1915, however, Britain's diplomats were shrewd and clever men. Time and again they skillfully avoided confrontation over the blockade issue. They did not want to offend the Americans, but their main objective was to gain American support for the Allied cause.

Soon, increasing commerce with the Allies compensated the U.S. many times over for the loss of trade with the Central Powers. Economic ties grew stronger every month between the Allies and the "Great Neutral."

GERMAN U-BOAT SINKS AN ALLIED MERCHANT SHIP IN BLOCKADE
OF BRITISH ISLES.
(LIBRARY OF CONGRESS)

Germany, too, saw the necessity to starve out Britain. Unable to block her ports with surface ships, the German navy launched an aggressive campaign of submarine warfare.

Unlike massive battleships, submarines were very small and frail. There was no room for cargo, so a submarine could stop a shipment only by sinking the ship. At first, when a U-boat sighted an enemy vessel, it would surface and fire a round from its one, small cannon as a warning. The passengers and crew were then supposed to evacuate the ship while the U-boat finished it off.

Some ships were faster than the underpowered U-boat and could escape while it was surfacing. Merchant vessels also began to carry large-caliber deck guns that could blow an exposed submarine out of the water. Therefore, surfacing was not only dangerous, but also deprived the U-boat skipper of his two best weapons: surprise and his torpedoes (which could be fired only while submerged).

In February 1915, Germany began unrestricted submarine warfare. Berlin announced that it considered the waters around the British Isles a "war zone." British ships would be sunk on sight, and the safety of neutral ships could not be guaranteed. The Germans made it clear that merchant vessels would be attacked without warning or regard for the fate of their crews.

On March 28, 1915, the first American life was lost in the sinking of a British ship. A month later, German airplanes attacked an American steamship, and on May 1, the U.S. tanker *Gulflight* was sunk by a torpedo. That same day, the *Lusitania* set sail. From New York to San Francisco the press condemned this "slaughter," "murder" and "piracy" of the Germans. Continued sinkings kept the public anger high. After the loss of the *Lusitania*, the *New York Times* reported "a grave crisis is at hand."

The sinking of the *Lusitania* had a profound effect on many Americans. German atrocities against civilians in Belgium and other occupied areas were fresh in the public mind. Together these horrors irreversibly damaged Germany's reputation and image. The American press began to portray the Germans as savage, barbaric "Huns."

Late in May the German government apologized about the two U.S. ships and said that they'd been attacked by mistake. Berlin even offered to pay for the loss of the *Gulflight*. Yet Germany made no excuse for the *Lusitania*. As a British ship, it had been fair game.

The president wanted to preserve America's neutrality. Yet he knew that he had to take a tough stand. He called these ocean ambushes a "violation of the sacred principles of justice and humanity." Wilson sent several stiff protests to Germany. The kaiser fumed but he, too, wanted to preserve America's neutrality. In September 1915, Berlin grudgingly called off the unrestricted U- boat campaign.

American neutrality was safe again. Yet just how neutral was America? The majority of Americans, including President Wilson, sympathized with the Allied cause. War relief groups raised money to send to French and Belgian refugees who had been displaced by the German advance. American banks made huge loans to Allied governments.

The kaiser had good reason to be upset. Germany's blockade of Britain had been provoked by Britain's blockade of Germany. President Wilson scorned Germany, but tolerated the British.

The United States was Britain's number one trading partner. Thus, the U-boats were also hurting American commerce. Many shippers would not risk sending their cargoes into submarine-menaced waters. This tied up business. During periods of peak U-boat activity, American ports became congested with tons of snarled freight. On U.S. docks, meat spoiled and produce rotted.

Not all Americans were pro-Allies. Many Irish-Americans, for example, came to the States because they could no longer tolerate Britain's longtime mistreatment of Ireland. They would be happy to see the British take a licking. Many German-American communities even raised money to send back to the Fatherland.

Even Americans sympathetic to the Allies believed that the United States should not in any way intervene militarily. Extending credit and trade with the Allies was one thing. Going to war on their behalf was quite another.

Pacifist demonstrations and movements sprang up across the nation. Most Americans clearly still cherished isolation. A popular song expressed the public attitude:

> I didn't raise my boy to be a soldier.
> I brought him up to be my pride and joy.
> To live to place a rifle on his shoulder.
> To shoot some other mother's darling boy . . .
> There'd be no war today
> If mothers all would say,
> I didn't raise my boy to be a soldier.

Secretary of State William Jennings Bryan privately favored Great Britain. Yet he and many others pressed for total non-involvement. He sponsored a ban on loans to countries that were at war, and urged the president to forbid American citizens from traveling on ships of warring nations. When Wilson rejected both of these sensible suggestions, Secretary Bryan resigned from the cabinet.

In December 1915 a delegation of American pacifists called The Peace Ship, headed by Henry Ford, sailed for Europe intent on ending the slaughter there. They believed that the greatest neutral nation owed it to humanity to try, at least. The belligerents' governments rejected the famous automobile manufacturer and his "peace pilgrims." Ford left Europe's inhospitable shores with a head cold five days after he arrived.

✭ 5 ✭

DEADLOCK: 1915

While Americans were busy avoiding war, the Europeans were trying to win one. On the Western Front, the year 1915 saw the opposing lines of trenches become stronger and deeper.

The French spent the year trying to liberate some of their country, only to learn the futility and costliness of massed infantry attacks against a well fortified trench line. France spent the lives of hundreds of thousands of her sons in useless efforts that only gained a few miles.

Meanwhile, the British had been building up their forces by drawing soldiers from every part of their far-flung overseas empire. By spring, Britain's forces in northern France numbered half a million men and were ready to take the offensive.

The German army struck first. It launched a major attack against the British line at Ypres, the city in northwest Belgium where the British army had been all but eliminated five months earlier. The 21 days of sheer slaughter that followed became known as the second battle of Ypres.

On the first day of the battle, April 22, 1915, the men in the British trenches could not have imagined the horror about to befall them, for on that day occurred a gruesome event in the history of warfare.

Sentries were peering through their rifle sights, watching for German infantry that they were told might be coming. Instead, they saw a greenish-yellow vapor rolling toward them from the enemy trench. Some who witnessed it said they were transfixed by its eerie beauty. Taking advantage of the westerly winds, the Germans had released a bank of deadly chlorine gas four miles wide.

The heavier-than-air gas cloud dipped into the Allied trenches. The soldiers in the trenches didn't know what hit them. Drawing chlorine gas into their lungs caused acute bronchitis, congesting their faces until they were livid purple and producing the most intense pain.

The left flank of the line broke and fled. This was a terrible mistake. By fleeing in the direction of the drifting gas, they prolonged their exposure. Running and gasping caused heavy breathing, which made them inhale even larger quantities of the deadly fumes.

The men of the right flank held their ground despite great suffering. (Many saved themselves by breathing through handkerchiefs soaked in their own urine, which helped to neutralize the gas.) Because of the courage of the men on the right flank, the Germans could not fully exploit the gap created on the left. Frustrated in the attempt to penetrate the Allied line, they called off the attack on May 13.

The use of poison gas and the excruciating pain it produced horrified Americans. Then, on May 7, came the news of the *Lusitania.* It seemed to the United States that the Germans were determined to give one proof after another that they were callous to the feelings of humanity and the esteem of civilized peoples.

The second battle of Ypres did more than introduce a fearsome new weapon, it gave birth to a new mode of military thinking. The Germans did not need the city of Ypres, but they knew the British would try to hold it at all costs. The goal of the German generals had not really been to gain territory, but rather to waste the strength of the British army, wearing them down, man by man. This ghastly strategy is called attrition.

There were many Americans who got to see the horror of the Western Front for themselves, young men and women who went there to serve as volunteers. Many worked for the American Red Cross. Another volunteer organization was the American Ambulance Corps. The ambulances were purchased and outfitted through fund-raising in the United States by private groups that supported the Allied cause.

Some Americans wanted to fight, even though their country was officially neutral. A way to get around that was to join the French Foreign Legion. (Made up of nationals from many countries, it asked only that a man obey its commanding officer.) As early as August 1914, a number of American men donned the red cap and blue overcoat of France's most famous colonial unit.

American volunteers were stunned by what they witnessed. Upon returning to the United States, they would give firsthand accounts of the war. Yet, words could scarcely describe the pitiful conditions of trench warfare.

Life was cheap in the trenches. Dead bodies were used to build support walls. Yellowing skulls and limbs could be seen packed into the dank, black soil. Everywhere lingered the smell of decomposing corpses, or the lime used to disinfect them.

Every day men lived in the presence of death. There might be a pair of boots lying in a trench—with the remains of feet still in them. No one would take any notice. Fat, well-fed rats scurried everywhere. It was said that they favored the eyeballs of the dead.

The filthy, overcrowded trenches were ideal breeding grounds for disease and parasites. Men were covered with lice and bugs. Many also suffered from "trench foot," cause by the dampness, in which they lost all sense of feeling in their feet.

Death could come suddenly, without warning, from a sniper's bullet, a grenade fragment or an artillery shrapnel. A direct hit by an artillery shell exploded a man into nothing, so that no traces of his body could be found. A shell might collapse a dugout roof, burying alive the men sleeping inside.

Also deadly were attacks from hand grenades, flamethrowers and poison gas. Both sides started to use chlorine gas on a large scale. Another

FRONT-LINE TRENCHES IN THE FOREST OF CHAUSSEAU, FRANCE.
(NATIONAL ARCHIVES)

chemical, phosgene gas, could seep through many of the crude masks then being worn. The Germans also developed vomiting gases. These made men sick so that they had to take off their masks, after which they could be attacked by other chemicals.

Trench life was relatively safe between big battles. For the men on both sides, the odds of surviving during a major attack were much slimmer. In an attack, the defending trench would first be pounded by an artillery barrage that would often last days without pause. This would "soften up" some of the defensive earthworks and obstacles. For the defending soldiers huddled in the darkness of their deep, damp dugouts for the duration, it was a nightmare from which they could not awake.

The constant shelling also deprived men of sleep and regular meals. This helped to reduce their effectiveness in combat. Some snapped under the pressure and went mad. Many were killed. Yet the majority survived. When it was over, the fatigued, deafened men would pop back up behind their machine-gun placements.

The moment the bombardment stopped, the infantry in the attacker's trench would go "over-the-top." The cratered, obstacle-covered strip between the friendly and enemy trenches was called No-Man's-Land. Men would form into long lines and move forward in waves at a walking pace.

It was always rough going. No-Man's-Land was pocked by thousands of shell holes, which were very often filled with water. Constant canon fire churned the landscape into a quagmire of muck and mud that sometimes literally swallowed men alive. As best they could the attackers would stumble forward. Fog, smoke or the steamed up goggles of their sweat-filled gas masks made visibility almost zero.

No-Man's-Land was stitched with barbed wire entanglements. The advancing infantry would try to penetrate the barbed wire through gaps that the artillery shells were supposed to have blown. Usually, few of these gaps could be found. The men would bunch up to go through. The enemy's machine-gun fire would concentrate on them, and the gaps would soon become clogged with bodies.

Some men would try to climb over the unbroken wire. Stuck on the sharp barbs, they would jerk around like flies in a gigantic spider's web, until enemy bullets riddled them.

Some would make it to the defenders' trench to face hand-to-hand combat. Others would take cover and crawl back to their own trench after

"NO-MAN'S-LAND," BETWEEN TWO DEADLOCKED ARMIES—
FRANCE, 1915
(NATIONAL ARCHIVES)

dark. Many wounded would be left for dead, moaning for days among the craters.

This was the horror of trench warfare. Once they had seen enough, American volunteers not enlisted in one of the armies could always go home. After all, it wasn't really their war. For Europeans, however, the war was inescapable, and it was just beginning to heat up.

After giving up the attack on Ypres in May, the German army went over to the defensive on the Western Front for the rest of 1915 so that large numbers of soldiers could be sent east. Austria-Hungary was proving to be a disappointing ally. She had again failed to beat the little Serbian army. Now the eastern part of its empire was being overrun by the Russians. Stiffened by the better-quality German troops, the Austrians were able to drive out the Russian army and crush Serbia completely.

In May 1915 Italy entered the war on the side of the Allies. Italian forces set out at once to attack Austria-Hungary. Their largely mountainous, common border, however, hindered open warfare and greatly favored the defense. To the misery of the Italian army, its unimaginative commander-in-chief was dedicated to the strategy of attrition. In June began the first battle of the Isonzo (after the Isonzo River). By the end of the fourth battle of the Isonzo in December the Italian army had lost over 280,000 men, the Austrian defenders about 160,000.

The war also saw a tragic sideshow that year in Turkey. The Allied armies and navies planned an amphibious invasion intended to knock the Ottoman empire (which had joined the Central Powers in November 1914) out of the war. Beginning April 25, 1915, an Allied force consisting of French, English, New Zealand and Australian soldiers landed on the Gallipoli Peninsula, situated about 100 miles southwest of Constantinople (Istanbul).

The Allied operation was an epic of confusion, mismanagement and bad timing. Also, the kaiser generously supplied German armaments and military advisers to the defending Turks, as well as one of his best generals to command them. After eight months of hard fighting, and 214,000 casualties, the Allied forces had not even advanced off the beachhead. In November the Allies decided to pull out. In a belated show of competence, they completed the evacuation by January 8, 1916, without losing a man.

✫ 6 ✫

ATTRITION: 1916

The beginning of 1916 saw the German army at the height of its success against the Russians on the Eastern Front. The German High Command decided, therefore, to renew its effort in the West. The chosen target would be the fortress-city of Verdun, in France.

There were certainly more strategic places at which to launch a major attack. France could afford to lose Verdun without jeopardizing its overall defensive position. The French, however, were emotionally attached to Verdun. It was one of their oldest and most sacred cities. Attila the Hun had burned the city in the fifth century. Now the "Huns" were back. This time France was determined to keep Verdun if it took every man she had.

This is precisely why the Germans chose it. They knew the French would try to hold it at all costs. The target was Verdun, but the goal was to inflict a mortal defeat on the French army by bleeding it white. The object was not to take ground, but to get as many men killed as possible. Once again, the tactic was calculated, cold-blooded attrition.

The battle began on February 21, 1916, with the most intense artillery barrage yet seen. Over the six-mile front more than two million shells rained down on the French defenders at the incredible rate of 28 per second. (Most contained high explosives, the rest, poison gas, which by this time was usually delivered by artillery fire.)

Soldiers on both sides marched into the furnace. Never before or since did so many die in so small an area—the inferno of hell itself to those that survived.

Of the returning soldiers, a French general wrote: "Their expressions . . . seemed frozen by a vision of terror: their postures betrayed a total dejection; they sagged beneath the weight of horrifying memories."

A German survivor wrote: "Verdun transformed men's souls. Whoever floundered through this morass full of the shrieking and dying . . . had passed the last frontier of life, and hence bore deep within him the leaden

World War I, the Western Front, 1914-1918

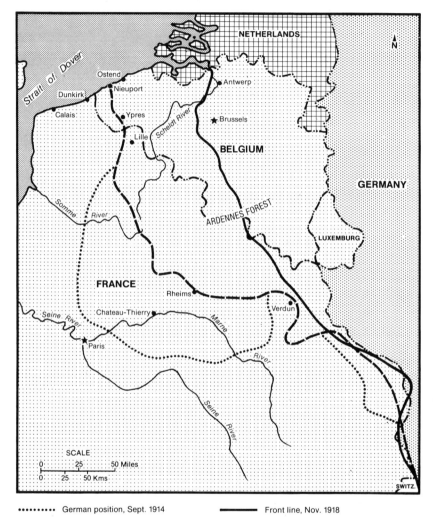

.... German position, Sept. 1914   ━━━━━ Front line, Nov. 1918

━ ━ ━ Nov. 1914-March 1918

memory of a place that lies between life and death." A French army chaplain recalled grimly: "Having despaired of living amid such horror, we begged God to let us be dead."

Nearly every unit of the French army took its turn at Verdun. The French systematically rotated fresh troops from "quiet" sectors and put them into the battle. Units that had already seen a lot of action would then be sent to man the quiet sectors. Soon, along almost every section of the Western Front were Frenchmen who had "done time" at Verdun. They were recognizable by their blank, empty expressions, and the hollow eyes that had seen too much.

A German soldier at Verdun predicted that the battle would continue "until the last German and the last Frenchman hobbled out of their trenches on crutches to exterminate each other with . . . teeth and finger-nails." It might have been so had events not forced the Germans to pull many troops out of the battle to fight elsewhere.

The British, determined to relieve pressure on the French army, launched a huge offensive along the Somme River, about 60 miles north of Paris. Months of careful and intensive preparation went into the planning of the operation. On June 24 began an artillery barrage that pounded the German positions for six days with a total of 1,508,652 shells.

At 7:28 A.M. on July 1, 1916, the Allied infantry went over-the-top. It was a catastrophe, the worst day in the history of the British army. On the average, something like 83 British soldiers were killed or wounded every minute. It was the most terrible one-day loss for any army during World War I. (The British army's dead and wounded for that single day numbered over 60,000—nearly a third killed in ac-tion—which was more than all the American soldiers killed during the entire Vietnam War.)

The British generals should have called off the offensive that night and cut their losses, but they were too stubborn to quit. In the first week, they advanced only a mile, and after a month, only two and a half miles.

Meanwhile, the Russians were doing their part to relieve the hard-pressed French at Verdun. In June they invaded eastern Austria-Hungary once again. It was Russia's final, desperate, all-out effort, but it achieved stunning success. Some 400,000 Austrians surrendered. Germany again had to send troops from the Western Front to save its ally.

In September, the British army surprised the Germans on the Somme front with a new secret weapon that was supposed to break the deadlock of trench warfare—the tank. Although the tanks performed well in a number of small-scale engagements, there were too few of them to make a difference.

By the end of October, the Russians had been driven from Austria-Hungary. The campaign had cost the Russian army a million men. In mid-November, the British finally gave up on the battle of the Somme. They had gained less than eight miles along a 12-mile front, at a price of nearly 600,000 casualties.

In mid-December, the battle of Verdun ended. The forts in front of the city, at last recaptured by the French, were useless mounds of rubble, with thousands of attackers and defenders entombed inside. The opposing lines were now roughly the same as they had been 10 months earlier. For this, about 950,000 French and German soldiers had been killed, wounded or captured.

Meanwhile, on the Southern Front, the Italian army had renewed its war of attrition against the Austrians. From April to November 1916 raged the 5th through 9th battles of the Isonzo. Little ground was taken but, as usual, casualties on both sides were enormous.

The Italian offensives, however, along with Russia's early success on the Eastern Front, convinced Rumania that Austria-Hungary would soon be defeated. In August 1916, Rumania joined the Allies. It was a fatal decision.

Once the Russians were in full retreat by October, Germany and her allies Turkey and Bulgaria dealt with the Rumanians. By December 1916, their country was completely overrun. Germany might not have been able to continue the war much longer had it not been for Rumania's vast supply of wheat and her rich oil fields, which the Germans now possessed.

The Allies did get some good news. Although World War I was fought mainly in Europe, there were many smaller battlegrounds around the world. In 1914, for example, all of Germany's possessions in east Asia were captured by British and Japanese forces. In Africa, some German colonial forces stubbornly resisted right until the end of the war. By 1916, however, the French and British had conquered most of Germany's African colonies.

Also in 1916 came good news from Allied troops fighting battles in Asia Minor against the Turkish Ottoman empire. British forces had gained ground in Mesopotamia and Arabia, while the Russian army pushed deep into Turkey itself.

Another battleground in 1916 was in the North Sea. On May 31 the German and British fleets ran into each other off Denmark's Jutland Peninsula. The battle of Jutland was the only major naval engagement of the war. Both sides claimed victory. In this clash, German gunners proved they were better shots, sinking twice as many warships as they lost (61,180 tons of German ships sank vs. 117,025 tons of British). Yet the German fleet would never leave port again.

As usual, the war in Europe was the big story for American newspapers throughout 1916. Not all of the fighting, however, took place on battlefields.

On April 23, a group called the Citizens Army took control of Dublin and declared Ireland's independence from the United Kingdom. They proclaimed it the Free Irish Republic and appointed a president. England quickly sent troops to stamp out what it called the Easter Rebellion. The American press blasted the English for this bloody act, calling them "tyrants" and "oppressors." American sentiment for Britain hit its wartime low.

That year the United States army made a few headlines of its own. On March 9, 1916, followers of the Mexican bandit and revolutionary Pancho Villa raided Columbus, New Mexico. Fifteen Americans were murdered and 13 wounded. President Wilson sent a 12,000-man military expedition 300 miles into Mexico to find Villa. The commander of the expedition, Brigadier General John J. Pershing, entered the public eye and became a hero.

Although Americans were temporarily distracted from the war, Germany managed to make its presence felt again. On March 24, 1916, a German submarine torpedoed the British liner *Sussex*, killing several American citizens. The incident brought the friction between Berlin and Washington to a head.

President Wilson, backed by Congress, issued an ultimatum to the kaiser. The U.S. government threatened to break off diplomatic relations with Germany if it did not comply. On May 4 the Germans gave in. They promised to abide by international law and not sink merchant and passenger vessels without attempting to warn them first.

The "Sussex pledge," as it was referred to, was not a very good formula for peace. Wilson's ultimatum made the issue of war or peace dependent on decisions made in Berlin. German military officials might decide that the submarine campaign was more important than the risk of American involvement in the war.

For a while it seemed to work. In November 1916, the president ran for reelection under the slogan "He Kept Us Out of War," and won by a narrow margin. Wilson would use the Sussex pledge as a token of the Germans' good faith, a trust they would soon break.

☆ 7 ☆

AN AMERICAN CRUSADE

Throughout the war President Wilson pressed for peace negotiations between the warring powers, without success. He also offered to mediate discussions. And in January 1917, with the war in its third year, the president made a final attempt to bring about peace talks.

Again he failed. It became apparent to Wilson that the governments on both sides would not settle for anything less than the total and unconditional surrender of the enemy. He gave up all hope that there could be a "peace without victory." But if one side must lose the war, Wilson was convinced that it should be the Central Powers.

If the Allies lost, it could be damaging to the United States economy. While the Europeans were preoccupied with killing each other, American commerce had benefited greatly. Its overseas trading surplus had increased from $690 million in 1913 to $3 billion in 1916. (The first three years of the war saw no less than 8,000 new American millionaires.)

The basis of this prosperity was the dependence of the Allied countries on American imports. Many of those imports were purchased with money the Allies were borrowing from American banks. By January 1917 the Allied debt stood at $2 billion. American business, therefore, had a stake in an Allied victory. Should the Allies be defeated, large American investments would be at risk.

There was also a deep concern among many Americans, including the president, over Germany's conduct during the war. Many saw the Allied cause as a crusade against German militarism. Yet many Americans still thought the United States should not have a political or military role in the outcome of the war.

President Wilson felt differently. He believed the United States must have a hand in shaping postwar peace. Like most Americans, he believed in the superiority of the American way and the corruption of the Old World. The war had revealed the disastrous consequences of the old diplomacy of secret treaties and intrigue. Wilson thought that the world was marching upward on an evolutionary path toward democracy, liberalism and open diplomacy.

A devout Presbyterian, Wilson believed that the years of horror and devastation caused by the war should be put to a higher end. It was as if the war was a transitional phase between the old order and a new and better world.

As war weakened the European powers, America emerged stronger. Wilson began to see the United States not as an ordinary mediator, but as an active peacemaker. He envisioned America as an architect with the power to construct a new world on the ruins of the old one.

True, Wilson had failed to use America's neutral position to bring the warring nations to the conference table. Now he realized that the United States could play a major role in a postwar peace conference only if it had helped to win the war. He began to consider military involvement on the side of the Allies.

Yet Wilson knew that it would take more than his lofty ideals about postwar peace and reconstruction to unite the country's many diverse ethnic groups behind the idea of American intervention. There could be no "hyphenated loyalty." German-Americans, Irish-Americans, Italian-Americans, Scandinavian-Americans—all Americans—would have to be galvanized into one nation, behind one cause.

Wilson knew that going to war would be a test of America's solidarity. (After all, he had won the election just two months earlier with a promise to keep the peace.) By the end of January, the president began thinking of how he could convince the American people that the United States should help defeat Germany. Then the Germans did the convincing for him.

On February 1, 1917, Berlin announced that it would resume unrestricted submarine warfare. The United States immediately broke off diplomatic relations with Germany. As one Allied ship after another sank, it was only a matter of time until an American ship was hit. It seemed to many people in the United States that war lay only one torpedo away.

Then an extraordinary development took place. British Intelligence intercepted a message from German Foreign Secretary Zimmerman to the German ambassador in Mexico City. The note urged Mexico to declare war on the United States if the U.S. sided with the Allies. It offered Mexico generous financial support and the return of its "lost territory" of Texas, New Mexico and Arizona.

It was a bizarre message. Mexico had no organized military power. Overrun by revolutionaries, it was a country on the verge of anarchy.

Wilson was outraged. He thought the message might have been a hoax, but Berlin clumsily admitted its authenticity.

On March 1, the Zimmerman telegram made headlines across the country. Its chief result may have been the elimination of the small minority in Congress that had opposed America's growing involvement with the Allies, but the public went wild. War fever heightened. Suddenly, the war in Europe seemed to be a clear-cut contest between good and evil.

On March 16, German submarines sank three American ships. Among them was the oil tanker *Illinois*, homeward bound to Texas. A large pair of American flags and the initials "U.S.A." were painted on its side. It had not been sunk by mistake. It had been stopped by a U-boat, boarded and plundered. Then the Germans destroyed it by setting off bombs in the oil compartments.

Former President Theodore Roosevelt thundered: "There is no question about going to war. Germany is already at war with us." Marchers took to the street carrying banners that read: "Kill the Kaiser!"—"On to Berlin!"—"Let's Get the Hun!"

On the night of April 2, 1917, a seething multitude formed outside the Capitol, while inside the president asked the Congress to declare war on the Central Powers. The packed gallery listened silently. Most of the congressmembers wore small "stars and stripes" on their lapels. The Supreme Court justices were also present. Chief Justice Edward Douglas White, a Civil War veteran, cried as he listened to the president's address.

"There is one choice we cannot make, we are incapable of making, we will not choose the path of submission," Wilson said. "It is a fearful thing to lead this great peaceful people into war, into the most terrible and disastrous of all wars, civilization itself seeming to be in the balance. But the right is more precious than peace, and we shall fight for the things which we have always carried nearest to our hearts."

One line from Wilson's war address people remembered most of all: "The world must be made safe for democracy." For many, this single sentence gave reason enough for America to enter the war.

The principles for which European governments were fighting were alien to the average American. But the triumph of democracy over dictatorship was an ideal that a nation of free men thought worth fighting for. So different was this truly American reason for war that Wilson made the symbolic gesture of calling the United States an "associate" rather than an ally.

PRESIDENT WILSON ADDRESSES A JOINT SESSION OF CONGRESS
AND ASKS FOR A DECLARATION OF WAR AGAINST GERMANY—
APRIL 2, 1917.
(LIBRARY OF CONGRESS)

On leaving the rostrum, he got the greatest ovation of his life. He was pleased, but his heart was heavy with sadness. Later, at the White House, he said to his secretary, "Think of what they were applauding. My message today was a message of death for our young men. How strange it seems to applaud that."

Congress reached its decision at 3 A.M. on April 6. Some lawmakers still held that America should stay neutral. When the voting came, the only congresswoman of that time, the pacifist Jeannette Rankin of Montana, whispered a gentle "no." (Twenty-four years later, on December 8, 1941, Rankin, back in Congress and still an isolationist at heart, cast the only "no" vote when the U.S. declared war on Japan.)

After a Senate vote of 82 to 6, the House voted 373 to 50 to support the president. The nation was at war.

☆ 8 ☆

CRISIS: 1917

The Allies were jubilant. America's long-awaited entrance into the war had finally come. Yet most Americans were not quite sure exactly what was expected of their country. The United States would, of course, continue to supply the Allies and loan them money. America's large navy could be of immediate help. A small, token expeditionary force would probably be sent to fight in France.

The Allies, however, were counting on the United States to send hundreds of thousands of men to fight on the Western Front. America was not at all ready for such a war. The country was physically unprepared to support its verbal declaration.

The United States Army in April 1917 was a quiet, sleepy institution where old soldiers killed time until they began drawing their pensions. It numbered less than 200,000 men. (Among the world's standing armies, it ranked only 17th.)

It was not much larger than King Albert's brave little Belgian army, and much less prepared to fight in a modern war. Its firearms were outdated. Its few cannon were antiques. Of its 55 airplanes, 51 were found to be hopelessly obsolete.

At first the United States did not recognize the scope of the job involved in mobilizing, training, supplying and transporting men, arms and equipment across the Atlantic. When President Wilson asked how many troops could be sent to France immediately, he was told 24,000 men—at most—with only a one-day supply of ammunition. America may have been ready to fight, but it was not "fighting ready."

This fact had not escaped the German High Command. Germany had long noticed American sympathy for the Allied cause. German military experts had made careful calculations of the length of time it would take the United States to achieve a stable war footing should it become involved. The minimum estimates were six to eight months. More likely it would take 12 months before America could put its full resources behind the war effort.

This period of security had given the Germans the confidence to resume unrestricted submarine warfare, which they knew would likely draw the United States into the war against them. It was a calculated risk. They knew that, if the tactic failed, American involvement would ultimately mean defeat for the Central Powers.

The Allies started the war with about 21 million tons of shipping, well over the minimum necessary to feed Britain and keep the armies supplied. Their shipbuilding program had not kept up with the loss rate from submarines. The Germans calculated that if their U-boats could sink 500,000 tons of shipping a month, Britain would be brought to its knees well before the United States got into full swing.

This mad policy nearly succeeded. The U-boats sank 540,000 tons of merchant shipping in February 1917, 578,000 tons in March and a

REVOLUTION BREAKS OUT IN RUSSIA, AFTER HEAVY WAR LOSSES AND A BREAKDOWN OF THE FOOD SUPPLY. RIOTING TROOPS AND CIVILIANS TAKE COVER FROM GUNFIRE, LEAVING DEAD AND WOUNDED IN THE STREETS.
(NATIONAL ARCHIVES)

strangling 874,000 tons in April. One in every four ships leaving British ports was sunk. Britain suffered crippling shortages. By May, there was enough food supply to last only six more weeks.

Germany, however, underestimated the effect of America's naval contribution. At Britain's most desperate moment, the U.S. Navy came to the rescue. Working together, the American and British fleets were able to cut monthly shipping losses in half by early fall of 1917.

On water, the Allies were beginning to turn the tables against Germany. On land, however, the Allies were in trouble. For them, 1917 would be the most critical and dangerous year of the war.

Discontent and unrest were reaching a climax in Russia. By January 1917, the Russian army had lost at least five million men, killed, wounded, captured and deserted. On the home front, the cost of living had increased seven times what it had been in 1914. Food supply to the cities had broken down. Workers everywhere went on strike. Troops and civilians began to riot.

On March 15, 1917, the Russian emperor, Czar Nicholas II, gave up his throne. A government of liberal aristocrats and politicians was formed. The new leaders wanted to keep up the fight against the Central Powers. The Russian army, however, was showing signs of severe strain. Just when the United States was joining the struggle against Germany, it looked as if Russia, a crucial ally, might soon be out of it.

The Allies now feared that Germany would be able to move hundreds of thousands of troops that had been tied down upon the Eastern Front to the Western Front. The French generals decided to gain ground while they still had the advantage. They made plans to launch a huge offensive.

The plan was to "pinch off" a bulge in the German line. Once surrounded, the defenders would be forced to surrender. It might have worked had the Germans not caught wind of the plan. The German army pulled back its line. The readjusted position was no longer an awkward bulge, it was now a death trap.

Despite pressure from the French government to reconsider the offensive, the French High Command chose to go ahead with the attack. On April 16, masses of French infantry went over-the-top—but not much further. In 10 utterly futile days, the French army lost another 187,000 men. The soldiers had taken more than they could stand, not from the Germans but from their own generals.

On April 29, a full-scale mutiny spread through the French army. Not less than 100,000 soldiers were later court-martialed. Some soldiers deserted over to the enemy. The stories they told about the extent of the mutiny seemed so incredible that the Germans did not believe them. As a result, Germany missed her best chance of the war for a decisive breakthrough on the Western Front.

In May, the French commander who had bungled the offensive was replaced by General Henri Pétain, a hero of the battle of Verdun. Pétain restored order and regained the confidence of the soldiers. He worked to improve their food and increase their leave time. Most of all, he promised them that there would be no new French offensive for the rest of the year. Pétain's strategy was summed up in one sentence: "We must wait for the Americans."

It was now up to the British to carry the Western Front. Eager to draw the Germans' attention away from the shaken French army, Britain's generals decided to launch a major attack. They chose for their offensive the wretched bogs and wetlands just east of Ypres in Belgium. Three years of war had churned the countryside around Ypres into one big, mangled mud pit. It was the sorriest possible ground for an operation.

Three miles south of the town, the Germans were poised menacingly on a crest called Messines Ridge. The British knew that before they could push east of Ypres they would have to take the ridge. The Germans had been there for two years and were well entrenched.

For months, English and Welsh miners, drafted into the Army for their digging skills, worked like moles to run tunnels under the German positions. Because the sudden appearance of mounds of dirt would give them away, every ounce of soil and chunk of rock had to be bagged and transported far to the rear.

In all, they dug five miles of tunnels, without being detected by the Germans. The tunnels were then packed with one million pounds of high explosives.

The blast that followed was so powerful that people as far away as London heard the rumble and felt the quake. Not only did it make history, but it changed geography. It made craters 100 yards across and 100 feet deep. More than 20,000 German soldiers were killed or maimed by the explosion.

After taking over what was left of Messines Ridge, the British prepared for the main assault. As usual, it was preceded by an intense bombardment lasting many days. While the British artillery "softened up" the battlefield, the weather did its share. Rain came down in torrents for days.

By the time the third battle of Ypres finally got under way on July 31, 1917, No-Man's-Land had dissolved into ooze. British soldiers had to advance through mud that was often up to their knees. Some men drowned in shell craters that had filled up with water. British tanks, stuck in the muck, were easy targets for German gunners.

Two years earlier, during the second battle of Ypres, the same field saw the first use of chlorine gas. The Germans now introduced by far the most terrible chemical—mustard gas.

Because it could penetrate clothing, gas masks gave only limited protection. It caused blindness, severe burns and large, festering blisters. Men were told not to touch the irritated areas, as it only made the burns spread, but victims often could not control themselves. They would scratch frantically and tear at the wounds until they had clawed themselves to death. Even today there is no adequate treatment for mustard gas wounds.

The battle raged on for more than three months until, finally, the British gave up the attack in November. It had not been the breakthrough the generals had hoped for. The British army had lost another 244,897 men to gain 9,000 yards of blood-soaked marshland.

While the British and Germans were slugging it out in Belgium, Italy made its last lunge at the Austrian line on the Isonzo sector. The 11th battle of the Isonzo (August 19–September 12) drained the Italian army's manpower, but brought the Austrian army to the very point of collapse.

Once more, Germany had to come to the rescue. The Austrians were beefed up with German troops released from the Eastern Front. The Austro-German force struck a sledgehammer blow at Caporetto. The Italians were overwhelmed.

The battle of Caporetto (October 24–November 12, 1917) was an unnerving disaster for the Allies. Italy lost 305,000 soldiers, 275,000 of whom had surrendered. What was left of the Italian army retreated 100 miles. Thousands of French and British troops, badly needed on the Western Front, were sent to Italy to check the enemy advance.

The Allies were clearly in a desperate position. Then, on November 7, 1917, the government of Russia was overthrown by Bolshevik Communists. The next day, the new Bolshevik government announced its plan to make a separate peace and, in December, it signed an armistice with the Central Powers.

Now, help from the United States was needed more than ever. Both sides waited, one with hope, the other with fear, for the arrival of the Americans.

⭐ 9 ⭐

MOBILIZING A NATION

You're in the Army now,
You're not behind a plow . . .
—Popular song of 1917

Having entered the war, the United States had the task of mustering its full resources behind the war effort as soon as possible. There was more to be done than raising an army. More ships would have to be built. Factories would have to be converted to manufacture armaments. Industry and agriculture needed to be reorganized to meet the demands of a wartime economy. "It is not an army we must shape and train for war," said the President, "it is a nation."

In the emotional fervor that followed the declaration of war on April 6, many young men rushed to volunteer for the armed forces. Yet, it was only a fraction of the number needed. After hearing three years of stories about the horrors of trench warfare, it is hardly surprising that more men did not run to join up.

President Wilson proposed national conscription, otherwise known as a "draft." Many members of Congress objected to the bill. The speaker of the House asserted that there was "little difference between the conscript [draftee] and the convict." "You will have the streets of our American cities running red with blood on Registration day," warned one senator.

Yet on May 18, 1917, Congress ratified the Selective Service Act, requiring all able-bodied males between the ages of 21 and 31 to register for active duty. Later in the war, the age limits were extended to include men from ages 18 to 45.

Surprisingly, there were no antidraft riots anywhere, not even, as had been expected, in the cities with large German-American populations. Some credit must be given to the secretary of war, Newton Baker, who enlisted the support of chambers of commerce and other local agencies "to make the day of registration a festive and patriotic occasion." The occasion did, in fact, go off more like a holiday than a grim mustering for war.

On the appointed day, June 5, 1917, 9,660,000 men registered. On July 20 came the first drawing of the "great national lottery." Blindfolded, Secretary Baker reached into a big glass bowl containing 10,500 numbers in capsules and pulled out number 258. In each registration district throughout the country the man holding number 258 was the first to be called into service.

PATRIOTIC POSTER ART ENLISTS IN THE CAUSE. THIS PORTRAIT OF UNCLE SAM BY JAMES MONTGOMERY FLAGG WAS SO POPULAR IT WAS USED AGAIN BY RECRUITING STATIONS IN WORLD WAR II.
(NATIONAL ARCHIVES)

The War Department designated 16 camps to be built in the North and 16 in the South. Each was near a railroad, on 8,000 to 12,000 acres of land with a good water supply. The southern camps were called "tent cities," mostly because they lacked wooden barracks. By contrast, the northern camps had some 1,200 buildings each.

It was the largest government undertaking since the building of the Panama Canal. It took 12 trains a day, each 50 cars long, to transport the construction materials. A veritable army of civilian workers was needed. Some 200,000 carpenters and other workmen (more than the combined strengths of the Union and Confederate armies at the battle of Gettysburg), labored continuously. They laid enough roofing to cover Manhattan and Atlantic City, with some to spare.

The fried steak and apple pie of the farewell party was still warm in their stomachs when the new recruits arrived to see the muddy, unpaved campsites that would be their new homes. Often the barracks were not yet ready. Many would have to sleep on the cold, wet ground, wrapped in blankets. Army chow, they found, was nothing like the food back home.

The winter of 1917–18 was particularly hard in the northern camps. For many of the southerners, it was their first time seeing snow. Measles, meningitis, influenza and pneumonia spread rapidly through the crowded camps. Many recruits died of disease.

Much equipment, artillery pieces in particular, was not yet available. New soldiers trained on wooden replicas of the weapons they would be using. Even uniforms were sometimes in short supply. At one camp, some soldiers were issued old, blue Civil War uniforms.

The men were given complete physicals, most for the first time in their lives. Many had never been to a dentist. It was probably not a pleasant first experience. Overworked Army dentists simply pulled out any tooth that looked like it might give trouble.

Some had never been to a doctor. Instruments for taking blood pressure or listening to the heart filled these men with fright. Vaccinations were the worst! One recruit recalled his first shots:

> As we went by, single file, the doctor would stick us with a long needle on the right arm. We had a little patch of iodine there, but the fellow in front of me was so frightened he forgot to move on after being stuck, and when the doctor turned around, he stuck the first brown spot that he saw with the result that the man got a double dose and nearly fainted. He fell

on the floor, everyone laughing at him . . . but I was next and did not feel like laughing much.

Underprivileged men from the rural South probably had the hardest time adjusting to camp life. Most of them had never had a hot shower or a full suit of clothes or shoes. Some did not know their left foot from their right. Many could not read or sign their name.

Some men came from places so remote that they had only a vague notion that they were citizens of the United States. Some did not know their birthdays or had only first names. Birthdates and last names were assigned to these men by the Army.

"THE BIGGEST DRUM IN THE WORLD" BEATS FOR A 1917 LIBERTY LOAN DRIVE IN NEW YORK, TO HELP FINANCE THE WAR THROUGH THE SALE OF U.S. TREASURY BONDS.
(NATIONAL ARCHIVES)

The camp instructors did their job of turning raw recruits into soldiers. The men learned to drill, shoot, dig trenches, lay barbed wire and construct latrines. They also learned that "kitchen police" (KP) did not mean guarding the kitchen.

Meanwhile, the government's primary concern was how to raise the tens of billions of dollars the war was going to cost. About one-third of the funds would come from new taxes on income, alcohol, tobacco and various other goods and services. The rest of the money would be borrowed from the people, through the sale of War Bonds.

Clubs and civic groups of all types, as well as federal and local government agencies, organized "Victory Loan" and "Liberty Loan" drives to encourage citizens to buy War Bonds. Popular stars of the infant movie industry, like Charlie Chaplin and Mary Pickford, made public appearances to urge Americans to invest in America's future through War Bonds.

ANOTHER PATRIOTIC POSTER BY JAMES MONTGOMERY FLAGG APPEALED TO AMERICANS' DEEPEST SENTIMENTS. (LIBRARY OF CONGRESS)

World War I gave birth to a centralized bureaucracy of unprecedented size. New federal agencies assumed unheard-of power. The War Industries Board, for example, took over raw materials and production and created new industries to meet war demands. The War Trade Board controlled imports and exports. The Federal Fuel Administration supervised efficient use of resources like coal and oil by industry and the public. Even the railroads were taken over and run by the government.

The Federal Food Administration was created to assure adequate food supplies for military needs and to send agricultural aid to the Allies. It monitored farm production and regulated prices. It asked Americans to plant "Victory Gardens" and observe "wheatless" and "meatless" days.

All this was the United States' first experiment with a government-directed economy. Some of the experts who staffed these wartime emergency boards would later use the valuable experience they gained to fight the economic Depression of the 1930s.

Public opinion, an intangible but important resource, also had to be mobilized. This was the mission of the most controversial of the new government agencies.

The Committee on Public Information hired hundreds of writers and artists who turned their talents to wartime propaganda. Pro-war leaflets and posters were widely circulated. The committee also sent skilled orators around the country to make speeches intended to rally the nationalistic emotions of the American people.

The spirit of "100% Americanism" promoted by the Committee had an ugly side effect. German-Americans, the country's largest single group of foreign-born citizens numbering 2.3 million at the time, became the target of partiotic frenzy. People of German origin felt the suspicion, scorn and hatred of their neighbors.

German-Americans tried to prove their loyalty with gestures like buying War Bonds and having the German language banned from school curriculums. They even changed the name of sauerkraut to "liberty cabbage." In spite of these efforts many German-American citizens were harassed. Thousands of German-Americans, who were not yet naturalized U.S. citizens, were arrested and placed in internment camps.

Mobilizing the nation for war was a painful growing experience. But America would emerge from it stronger and more united than ever before.

☆ 10 ☆

THE BATTLE OF THE ATLANTIC

The Allies were pleased with the energy America was putting into its mobilization in the spring of 1917. However, an army in North America was of no use to them if the kaiser made good his promise to block the Atlantic sea lanes. Germany was counting on her U-boats to sink American troop ships before they could land in Europe. Unless the battle of the seas was won, the war on land would be lost.

An effective anti-sub tactic was the convoy. In a convoy, the most important vessels, the loaded troop transports, were surrounded by smaller, fast-moving combat ships called destroyers. Destroyers were designed and equipped to attack submerged submarines.

Also, by sailing on the outside of the convoy, a destroyer could, if necessary, block a torpedo with its own hull. The idea was that it was better to lose a destroyer than a huge transport with its tons of supplies and many hundreds of soldiers.

Because the naval war was to be directed against submarines, the Navy suspended the building of battleships. Instead, it planned construction of 250 more destroyers. It also planned to build 400 smaller boats called submarine chasers.

American scientists developed simple underwater listening devices, the forerunner of today's sonar. Munitions experts developed effective depth charges. These were canisters of TNT that could be hurled into the water from the deck of a destroyer and set to explode at various depths.

Many of the new ships were still under construction when the war ended. Even so, the Navy by then had 834 combat vessels on convoy duty. The overall strength of the U.S. Navy in 1918 reached some 2,000 ships and 533,000 men.

The first U.S. Navy vessels to see wartime service were 34 destroyers sent to Queenstown, Ireland, in May 1917 and stationed there. From this base they went out on convoy duty.

In November 1917 two of the destroyers from Queenstown forced the surrender of the German submarine *U-58*. In most cases, however, destroyers fired their deck guns and dropped depth charges until they thought their prey was sunk. But there was never any certainty that an enemy sub had been destroyed. Sailors could only search the waves for floating bits of debris or an oil slick, which they optimistically interpreted as another U-boat sent to the bottom of the ocean.

One seaman, William Duke Jr., described his experience on a cruise in December 1917:

> *We were caught in a gale . . . and the seas were breaking over us. We were crawling around on deck . . . looking for a hatch cover that had become unfastened. We suddenly discovered that six depth charges had become unloosed and were lurching about, butting the bulkworks with every roll of the ship.*
>
> *These depth charges are controlled by the paying out of wire and when a certain amount becomes uncoiled, they automatically explode. As no man knew how much the wire had become unmeshed, we all had to work fast, heaving them overboard. They went 'pop, pop, pop' as quickly as champagne corks at the French Ball. How we ever escaped blowing off our own stern is still regarded as a miracle by us all.*

A little later they reached the spot where a U-boat had surfaced and was firing its deck gun at a sailing vessel. As Duke's destroyer approached, the submarine submerged.

> *We were soon amid the rushing of turbulent water that is caused by a sub directly after submerging. We let go one [of the remaining depth charges] set to explode at about 80 feet deep . . . We were soon rewarded by seeing the color of the water change [to black] in the immediate vicinity of the explosion.*

Duty on convoy destroyers was characterized by days and days of boredom. Such days could be broken at any second by moments of tense, heart-stopping excitement at the appearance of an enemy submarine or torpedo trail.

Yet even the quiet times could be very unpleasant. In rough seas, seamen could sleep only by bracing themselves in their bunks. Men on duty became exhausted from constant holding on to lines or ladders. Then there was the danger of the ship capsizing in the heavy swell.

Wind, rain and cold added to the sailors' discomfort. The winter of 1917–18 was a particularly bitter one on the North Atlantic. The Navy vessels steamed into port looking more like icebergs than ships.

Life ashore at Queenstown was a relief, but not without its troubles. The American sailors were not always on the best of terms with the Irish at the nearby town of Cork. The assistant secretary of the navy, Franklin Delano Roosevelt, went to visit the base. Years later, when he was president, he recalled:

> *The young ladies [of Cork] . . . preferred the American boys and, of course, the young gentlemen of Cork didn't like that . . . They staged a raid on our seamen. There being about 1,000 civilians, they drove our men back to the train. [The sailors] came back with a good many broken heads. Liberty [off-base passes] . . . was suspended until the Mayor of Cork gave assurance that the town people would behave better next time.*

Roosevelt also remembered inspecting one of the machine bays aboard the U.S.S. *Melville.* He noticed a large canvas covering something. Beneath the canvas Secretary Roosevelt found "the finest assortment of brass knuckles and pieces of lead pipe that you ever saw." He turned to a large, redheaded chief petty officer by the name of Flanagan and asked him what they were for. Flanagan saluted and said: "Sir, that's for the next liberty trip to Cork, damn these Irish."

Not all Navy ships were on convoy duty. There were a number of battleships that joined the British blockade against the German fleet. For American seamen, life on the huge battleships not only was considerably more comfortable, but also offered less opportunity for excitement. There was little chance that the German warships, now outnumbered two to one, would appear.

Another sort of duty was aboard minelaying ships operating out of Scotland. Their mission was to lay a field of mines from Scotland all the way across the North Sea to Norway. That's about the same distance as from New York City to Washington, D.C. This was to be strictly an American project. In all, the Navy laid 70,000 mines (each with 300 pounds of TNT), which blew up at least eight submarines.

Minelaying also had little excitement or glory, but it was hard work. There were dangers, too. In rough weather there was the risk of hitting a mine already laid. A ship might suffer, as one seaman put it, "some of our own particular brand of punishment."

Life on a submarine chaser was no less hazardous, but somewhat more exciting. American submarine chasers mainly patrolled waters in the Mediterranean Sea. They took part in many submarine hunts. According to one skipper, whose boat was stationed at the Greek island of Corfu: "Words cannot express the life on the chasers. . . . They are small but mighty. They ride worse than a horse or a mule and rock and roll like a cradle."

Life was even more uncomfortable aboard the fairly crude and fragile American submarines. They were used for the treacherous and difficult work of counter-submarine warfare.

The Navy had many tasks. They all led to one purpose—getting transports and merchant ships past the lurking U-boats to the European harbors. In this way the Navy played a vital role in the war effort.

★ 11 ★

CONVOY TO FRANCE

AMERICAN TROOPS EMBARK FOR FRANCE—1917.
(NATIONAL ARCHIVES)

Before America's new army could fight in France, it had to cross an ocean. Troops from training camps across the country funneled into embarkation ports along the east coast. From New York, Boston, Norfolk, Charleston and others, they set sail. They went on large, fast transports, and sometimes on old, slow tubs. Whatever the ship, it always sailed as part of a convoy, which steamed at the pace of the slowest ship.

Aboard the crowded ships, the men tried to stay above deck as much as they could. They amused themselves by playing cards and organizing wrestling matches. For most of them, it was their first time at sea. Many became seasick and some could hardly eat anything for the whole trip.

In more than one sense, the enlisted men and their officers were literally in the same boat. As one recruit put it: "It gives the bucks [privates] a guilty joy to know that bars and stripes [of high rank] are no protection against seasickness. Another evidence of the democracy of our army is that it doesn't matter whether an officer or soldier goes overboard—the ship won't stop in either case."

Most trips were happily uneventful for the troops. But they always took precautions. Lifeboat drills were a daily exercise. After dark, no lights were allowed on deck, even smoking was prohibited. In danger zones, everyone slept in their clothes and life preservers.

Most of the troops believed that their passage would be a safe one. They put their trust in the new defensive tactics. The ships moved in a zig-zagging pattern, which made it harder for U-boats to aim their torpedoes. Ship hulls were painted with camouflage patterns that made them difficult to see clearly from submarine periscopes. Most of all, the men felt confident that the accompanying destroyers would keep them from harm.

There were many false alarms. Periscope sightings often turned out to be a piece of driftwood or a reflection on the water. But sometimes these "sub scares" were real submarines.

Just after dark, on February 5, 1918, a torpedo struck the troop ship *Tuscania*. The 2,500 men on board scrambled to get on deck. Unlike the passengers of the *Lusitania*, these men had rehearsed many times for precisely this emergency. They carefully lowered the lifeboats and evacuated the rapidly sinking vessel in good order. Very few lives were lost.

Fortunately, and to the U.S. Navy's credit, the *Tuscania* was the only Europe-bound troop transport to be sunk. There were, however, a number of very close calls. In June 1918, the *Von Steuben* narrowly missed being sunk. The *Von Steuben* was one of a number of German ships, trapped in American ports since 1914, that the U.S. Navy promptly seized when Congress declared war.

The *Von Steuben*'s lookout spotted the foamy, white trail of a torpedo heading directly toward them. Within an instant, he alerted the bridge. The captain gave orders for evasive action. The crew, acting without hesitation or confusion, maneuvered the ship. The men held their breath as the cigar-shaped engine of death skimmed by, missing the bow by a bare 20 feet.

The commander of convoy operations, Vice Admiral Albert Gleaves, commented later, "Here was a case where three brains acted quickly and in coordination, the lookout, the captain and the helmsman. The slightest mistake on the part of any one of the three would have resulted in the loss of the ship."

Priority was given to loaded troop transports. After their men and cargo were safely landed, convoys sometimes had to return to the United States without destroyer escorts. On May 30, 1918, the German submarine *U-90* sighted an unescorted convoy of four ships sailing back from France. The U-boat attacked. Three of the ships got away. The fourth and largest of the ships, the *President Lincoln*, sank after taking three torpedo hits.

Soon after, *U-90* surfaced and approached the survivors' rafts and lifeboats. The German skipper tried to find the ship's commander, Captain P.W. Foote, but he had disguised himself as a sailor. The men assured the U-boat commander that Foote had gone down with the ship. Noticing the officer uniform of a Lieutenant Isaacs, the German skipper ordered him aboard, then submerged and sailed away.

The next morning, two U.S. destroyers arrived on the scene. Picking up the survivors was slow and risky work. A U-boat might be waiting nearby, using the lifeboats as bait for new victims. The rescue took four hours to complete. Only 26 men were lost out of the 785 that had been aboard.

Shortly after the last man was pulled out of the water one of the destroyers spotted *U-90*'s periscope. The destroyers headed straight for the submarine at top speed and dropped depth charges where it was spotted.

Lt. Isaacs, prisoner aboard *U-90*, learned firsthand what it was like to be attacked by an American destroyer. "We felt depth bombs exploding all about us," he wrote months later, in an official report. "I counted 22 bombs in four minutes; five of them very close." The German skipper barely saved his vessel by quickly diving 200 feet, turning off the engines and "playing dead."

U-90 returned to port in Wilhelmshaven, Germany. Lt. Isaacs was sent to a prisoner of war camp. After persistent effort he managed to escape and made his way to Switzerland. He was then brought to the British Admiralty in London, where he gave a full report about all that he had learned about the operation of U-boats.

In September 1918, a submarine torpedoed the crowded troop transport *Mount Vernon*. Only one torpedo hit, but it blew a 19-foot hole in the transport's side and flooded half the boiler rooms. The escorting destroyers first laid a massive screen of black smoke to hide the stricken vessel. Then they fanned out and began dropping depth charges.

Meanwhile, the *Mount Vernon* had all it could do to stay afloat. Sailors worked feverishly to stop the flooding and keep the remaining boilers going. The soldiers on board had work, too. They formed a bucket line and bailed out water for the next 18 hours until the ship finally reached port in France.

Experiences like these were exceptional on the seas. Only 71 of the more than two million American soldiers transported across the Atlantic in 1,142 troop ship sailings were lost. Few troops encountered any hazard worse than seasickness.

The Navy had achieved a miracle in the face of ever present danger from beneath the waves. It assembled a "bridge of ships" that transported not only a huge army to France, but also an average of four tons of supplies and equipment for each soldier. It won the Atlantic battle. This was an essential prelude to winning the great battles on the Western Front.

✳ 12 ✳

OVER THERE

The first American troops arrived in France on June 28, 1917. To the tired French people, exhausted by three years of attrition, these fresh young men brought promise and new hope.

The "doughboys," the nickname (of disputed origin) of the American soldiers, had come to fight on the side of liberty. Many thought it repayment of the debt owed to France for having helped their forebears win the American Revolution.

On July 4, 1917, the city of Paris threw a hearty welcome for the doughboys. During the celebration, an American colonel named C.E. Stanton uttered four words that were to stir both the French and American nations: "Lafayette, we are here." (Stanton was referring, of course, to the French general who fought for the United States during the War of Independence.)

These first men were the nucleus of what would become a huge army called the American Expeditionary Force (AEF). General John "Black Jack" Pershing, of the Mexican expedition, was the man President Wilson chose to be commander-in-chief of the AEF.

Pershing was born in Missouri in 1860 into a family whose original, German name was Pfoersching. In 1886 he graduated from the United States Military Academy at West Point, top of his class. While serving in the U.S. Cavalry, he fought in the last Indian Wars of the American West.

In those days, promotions in rank were painfully slow. By his mid-thirties he was still a lieutenant. He considered leaving the Army to become a lawyer. His good friend Charles Dawes, future vice president of the United States (1925–29), convinced Pershing to stick with the Army a while longer. Neither of them could have dreamed that Pershing's Army career would skyrocket him to international fame.

In 1898 Pershing fought in Cuba where he won the Silver Star. Next he went to the Philippines to help put down the Moro rebellion. Only a captain, Pershing won the admiration of President Theodore Roosevelt, who sent him to act as an observer in the Russo-Japanese War of 1904–05.

Roosevelt rewarded Pershing in 1906 by elevating him four ranks to brigadier general. Pershing, only 46 years old, had jumped over 862 senior officers, creating considerable bitterness among his fellow officers for many years.

Pershing's devotion to duty helped him to weather personal hardship. The day he arrived in Texas to lead the Mexican expedition, he received the news that his wife and three small daughters had burned to death in a fire at the Presidio Army base in San Francisco. Pershing went on with his mission and proved himself an able leader of men. When he returned, President Wilson made him a two-star general.

Wilson probably could not have made a better choice for commander of the AEF. Pershing was no great strategist and often lacked military wisdom. Yet, he had patience, emotional balance and unshakable fortitude—important qualities if one is to shape an army. Pershing's organization of the AEF from scratch was one of the great feats of World War I.

Pershing was the picture-perfect image of an indomitable high commander. His height and rigid posture seemed tailor-made for monuments. He possessed a strength of character that inspired confidence in his men as well as his political superiors in Washington.

Most of all, Pershing had the grit and determination to stand up to the Allied governments and their generals. France and Britain were not interested in an independent and untested American Army. They needed men to bolster their thinned-out lines. They wanted to use American manpower to flesh out their depleted units.

Pershing said no. He was appalled by the callous disregard the Allied generals had for the lives of their troops. Casualties were just numbers to them. Pershing could not bear the thought of his men being dragged into some wasteful trench battle at the whim of foreign generals whom he considered to be incompetent strategists.

Not only was Pershing going to keep his Army intact and independent, he also intended to keep it away from the fighting until he felt it was fully trained. The Allies constantly pressured him to commit his troops, ready or not. They even put severe pressure on the American government to remove Pershing, but Wilson doggedly stuck by his general.

Pershing realized that the stateside training his men had received was inadequate for the kind of war that faced them at the front. New training areas were set up in the rear.

GENERAL PERSHING ARRIVES IN FRANCE.
(LIBRARY OF CONGRESS)

French troops, hardened veterans loaned to Pershing, became professors to the green Americans. The French instructors could hardly believe how ill-trained the doughboys were. Yet, in time, they were amazed by the speed and dedication with which these same Americans applied their new training and tactics.

In early October, Pershing arranged with General Pétain, commander-in-chief of the French army, to have small American units go into the French line for 10 days at a time for the sake of experience. Through this rotation system, most doughboys would be initiated into trench warfare.

The line around the city of Toul was the spot Pershing chose for the first rotations. This was one of the so-called "quiet sectors." Except for occasional shelling, sniping and trench raids, there had been no fighting there since 1914. Both sides seemed content to keep it that way.

Pershing chose this sector so his men could gain confidence without the risk of getting caught in a major attack and being mauled or beaten. A few weeks later the Germans discovered that the virgin American troops were now in the line. They decided to send a welcoming committee for the new arrivals.

At midnight on November 2, 1917, German infantrymen staged a well-executed raid on the American trench. After a short barrage, the

Germans cut through the wire without being detected and infiltrated the American position. They did their bloody work and got away.

The Germans killed three doughboys and took 11 prisoners. Corporal Nick Mulhall had the unpleasant distinction of being the first U.S. soldier of the war to be captured. He was never seen or heard from again.

The raid was intended to humiliate the Americans and shake their morale. Far from it, the United States now had three heroes to rally around, and the doughboys were eager to retaliate.

Thereafter, trench raids were frequent on both sides. On one occasion, Private Leslie Lane turned a corner and was confronted by a group of soldiers. Lane ducked down to get a better view of them against the dark night sky.

"I was asked in French if I would consent to become a prisoner," he recalled. "I thought it was one of our French friends fooling around . . . The questioner then asked me in quite fluent English."

Lane stepped forward to see that it was a German sergeant-major with a party of about 15 men. The big German grabbed Lane and tried to silence him. "I then kicked the fellow in a vulnerable spot so furiously," recalled Lane, "that it brought him to his knees."

Lane then shot the sergeant-major before he himself was knocked unconscious. The shot alerted the other Americans and the rest of the raiders scattered back to their line. Lane soon came to, only to feel the German sergeant-major quivering at his feet.

"I reached to get a hold of him so I could get up first, and in doing so, found that he had pulled the pin from a 'potato masher' grenade, which exploded as I grabbed his hand, shattering three fingers on my left hand."

Another soldier, who saw this, reported that Lane had been killed. As Lane struggled to crawl to a first aid station, an American sentry turned the corner.

"Knowing there were Germans around and thinking I was killed, he was taking no chances and made a lunge for me with his bayonet. I saw the gleam of the bayonet aimed at my throat and raised my injured hand to ward off the blow."

The bayonet mangled his hand even more. The sentry then realized it was Lane and apologized profusely. "But I had no time to listen," recalled Lane, "as I was bleeding to death and wanted to get to First Aid before it was too late."

The enthusiasm and vigor of the doughboys was refreshing to the tired Allied soldiers. The patriotic songwriter George M. Cohan put the spirit of the Americans to music. His most famous tune could be heard in every Allied trench, dugout and gunpit on the Western Front. French, British and American soldiers sang it while cleaning their guns. They whistled it while marching. They hummed it while they munched their hard biscuits and creamed beef.

> Over there, over there,
> Spread the word, send the word, over there,
> That the Yanks are coming, the Yanks are coming,
> The drums drum drumming everywhere.
> So prepare, say a prayer.
> Send the word, spread the word to beware,
> We'll be over, we're coming over,
> And we won't come back till it's over over there.

By the end of 1917, the AEF was becoming a sizable, well-trained force. (Pershing was promoted to four-star general, the first one since the Civil War.) The Allies began to feel that they were past the danger zone and that now it was just a matter of time until the war was won.

The Germans, however, had some deadly surprises left in store for the Allied armies.

☆ 13 ☆

THE NEW STORM

THE GERMAN HIGH COMMAND: KAISER WILHELM II, WITH
HINDENBURG AND LUDENDORFF AT EITHER SIDE, EACH WITH
ONE HAND IN POCKET, AS WAS CUSTOMARY IN THE PRESENCE OF
THE KAISER, WHOSE LEFT ARM WAS PARALYZED FROM BIRTH.
(NATIONAL ARCHIVES)

The first two months of 1918 were calm ones on the Western Front. They were too calm. The Allies began to wonder what the German army was up to. By mid-March, Allied intelligence confirmed that something big was going on. With remarkable secrecy, the Germans were massing incredible amounts of troops, artillery, ammunition and other equipment in preparation for a lightning offensive that would stun the world.

The German High Command reasoned that an all-out push in the west might knock the Allies out of the war before Pershing could fully organize the AEF into an independent fighting force. With tens of thousands of Americans arriving in France every week, the Germans knew that the time for attack was now or never. It was a desperate gamble, Germany's last hope for victory.

The British Fifth Army held a 41-mile line that started south of Arras and ran down to Soissons, where the British and French lines joined. The German plan was to crush the Fifth Army and drive a wedge into this sector. They believed that the British would fall back toward their supply bases on the English Channel—away from Paris. The French, the Germans assumed, would pull back to protect their capital. Thus a gap would exist, through which German troops could pour.

The commander of the British Fifth Army, General Sir Hubert Gough, had seen the blow coming and made what preparations he could. General Pershing had loaned him three U.S. Engineer Regiments to help him with his defenses. Afterwards, the engineers fought with the Fifth as infantry, the first Americans to see full-scale warfare since the Civil War.

Gough had summoned his division leaders earlier that week for a pep talk. Interestingly, the British general ended by quoting Abraham Lincoln: "We accept this war for one object, a worthy object, and the war will end when that object is attained. Under God, I hope it will never end until that time."

Although Germany had been slow to build tanks, its generals had found another answer to trench warfare. They used specially trained shock units called *sturmtruppen* (literally, "stormtroopers"). They would filter forward under artillery cover and pierce the enemy's line of defense at a number of selected weak points. The strongest points would then be cut off and surrounded and could be dealt with later by other troops coming up behind.

Operation Michael, as the Germans called it, began at 4:50 A.M on March 21, 1918, with a massive bombardment. The British waited for the attack that they knew would follow. They expected solid lines of men walking into the slaughter as was usually done. Instead, the stormtroopers dashed forward, concealed by gas and fog, and slashed into the British line. The new tactics caught the British by surprise. The Fifth Army collapsed. All British reserves had to be rushed in to plug the gap.

The German army struck again around Ypres on April 9. Here the British were better prepared. The Germans made only modest gains, at great cost. After 20 days of hard fighting, they gave up the attack. The German army's next blow, however, fell on the French in the hilly region between Soissons and Rheims, on May 27. It smashed through their defenses.

This sector had been considered "safe" by the French high command. Only the most battered units, some less than half strength, had been stationed there. They had been sent there from more active parts of the front to rest and recuperate.

In just eight days, the Germans advanced 35 miles, more than all the Allied offensives of the previous three years put together. Along the way, the Germans captured much equipment and 65,000 prisoners.

Not since 1914 had the Allied situation been so precarious. The enemy was on the Marne River again, only 37 miles from Paris. The capital was gripped with panic. The French government had packed up and was ready to move to Bordeaux in southwest France.

French General Ferdinand Foch, who had just been made Supreme Allied Commander, had committed almost all remaining reserves to the sector under attack, but was unable to stem the German advance. The overwhelmed reinforcements, said Foch, "evaporated immediately like drops of rain on a red hot iron." Not since 1914 had Allied hopes of victory seemed so remote.

On May 30, Foch sent General Pétain, commander in chief of the French army, to General Pershing, to ask in person that American troops be sent to the danger point. Pétain had reviewed the situation in detail. He told Pershing that it was doubtful that France could survive the loss of Paris. It was not only the spiritual heart of the nation, but also an important industrial center and the focal point of all the major railroad systems.

Pershing listened respectfully to the French general, but was reluctant to comply with his request. Of the half-million American soldiers then in Europe, only four divisions were ready for combat. Two of these had already been pushed into the French line and had seen limited action. If he loaned France more troops it would delay for weeks the plan for an independent American Army.

He also knew the situation was critical. There was no choice. He agreed to put the U.S. 2nd and 3rd Divisions at Pétain's disposal.

The 2nd Division, which included a brigade of U.S. Marines, had been stationed in a quiet region northwest of Paris. Commanded by Lieutenant Colonel Frederick Wise, this was the only Marine brigade on the Western Front. Now they headed out for the front as fast as they could along clogged roads. In the last week, these roads had become a tangle of wounded troops, supply trucks, animals and civilian refugees fleeing the advancing Germans.

Vietnamese drivers (from French Indo-China) were assigned to transport the 2nd Division, and had been on the road almost nonstop for 72 hours. Exhausted, several fell asleep at the wheel, killing and injuring American passengers.

It was dusk by the time the first battalions of doughboys arrived at Sixth French Army headquarters. The French commanding officer did not know what to do with them. The front was in such flux that danger came from a dozen points at once. Where was the main German blow going to fall? French intelligence had broken down, unable to cope with the rapid movements of open warfare.

The French decided to rush the Americans into the line piecemeal, by companies, as had been done with France's own reinforcements. Colonel Preston Brown, 2nd Division chief of staff, refused to consider this. The 2nd Division must fight as a unit, he insisted, on a defensive line supporting the French. First, stop the German spearhead, then counterattack. That was the only sensible plan.

Sixth Army headquarters was uneasy about entrusting a section of the line to the raw, inexperienced troops. How could they stand up against tough, disciplined German stormtroopers? Colonel Brown indignantly replied, "These are American regulars. In 150 years they've never been beaten. They will hold."

Despite orders to the contrary, French units continued to give ground. They filtered back across fields waist-high in bright-green winter wheat, past deserted farms and villages. Many tried to retreat in orderly fashion, fighting as they went. Others fled in panic, leaving a trail of discarded equipment for the enemy to gather and distribute among its own troops.

By noon on June 2, Lieutenant Colonel Wise's battalion of Marines had moved into position and was digging in. Because entrenching equipment had not yet arrived, the men had to dig with bayonets, mess kits and spoons. Although there were still a few French units between them and the enemy, they wasted no time. The Germans were already shelling their position with artillery.

The Marines waited in their pits. They were hungry. The mobile field kitchens were still far behind. The only food around was French rations, mainly cans of Argentine corned beef called "monkey meat" by the troops. But the beef had spoiled before being canned. Famished as they were, the Marines could not gag down the putrid meat product.

DOUGHBOYS TAKE COVER FROM GERMAN SHELLING.
(NATIONAL ARCHIVES)

By late afternoon the last French unit marched by. Their commanding officer went up to one of Wise's company commanders and said that there were orders for everyone to retreat. "Retreat, hell!" barked Marine Captain Lloyd Williams. "We just got here!"

Soon after the blue-uniformed Frenchmen disappeared to the rear, the German bombardment grew more intense. From the woods on the Marines' right front, German machine guns opened up. Two columns of enemy infantry fanned out into the field.

Colonel Albertus W. Catlin, commanding the 6th Marine Regiment, recorded an enthusiastic description of what took place in a book he wrote after the war called *With the Help of God and a Few Marines*:

> *If the German advance had looked beautiful to me . . . that metal curtain that our Marines rang down on the scene was even more so. The German lines did not break, they were broken. . . . Three times they tried to reform and break through that hail of lead, but they had to stop at last. The U.S. Marines had stopped them. Thus repulsed, with heavy losses, they retired, but our fire was relentless; it followed them to their death.*

Although it was only a short, small-scale skirmish, Wise's battalion had stopped the Germans at their closest point to Paris since 1914. Back in America the Marine Corps became the toast of the nation. After the news of this engagement hit the papers, Marine enlistments rose 100% in two days.

Defending a dug-in position was one thing, however. It remained to be seen how well the Americans would do when the order came to counterattack.

IDEALIZED MARINE GRACES ANOTHER JAMES MONTGOMERY FLAGG POSTER.
NATIONAL ARCHIVES

★ 14 ★

DEVIL DOGS OF
BELLEAU WOOD

The French Sixth Army now planned a major counterattack to begin the morning of June 6. The point of the German spearhead was a quarter-mile east of the Marine position in a kidney-shaped patch of trees called Belleau Wood.

The Marine brigade was ordered to take control of Belleau Wood while the 167th French Division seized an expanse of wheat fields on the high ground northwest of the wood. French Intelligence assured the American commander that it was "lightly held and you should have no trouble capturing it."

The Germans assigned Hans Otto Bischoff, a 46-year-old major, to direct the defense of Belleau Wood. He spent three days carefully preparing his positions. The one-square-mile Belleau Wood was an old hunting preserve about half the size of New York's Central Park. Major Bischoff had turned it into a huge machine-gun nest. The Marines soon called it "Hellwood."

In all, Bischoff had carefully positioned 200 machine guns. He arranged the machine-gun nests in such a way that if one was captured, it would be exposed to flanking fire by two others. There were also three elaborate lines of trenches, protected by barbed wire, mortar teams and by sharpshooters in rifle pits.

Bischoff had done his job well, but his men were not in the best shape. For months they had been surviving on a diet of black bread, barley and dried vegetables. Many were down with the flu and dysentery. Nevertheless, he believed his Germans would stop anything the Americans could throw against them.

The French 167th Division attacked on schedule. The troops advanced well and drove the Germans from several entrenched positions. However, the French artillery did not lengthen its range fast enough. Its barrage fell on its own advancing troops and caused many casualties. Getting hit from behind by their own guns and in front by the enemy proved too much for the French infantry. The shaken, confused Frenchmen retreated to their start line.

The Marines had difficulties of their own. A company under Captain Orland Crowther was ordered to take Hill 142, north of the wood, to protect the left flank. They were pinned down for hours by heavy machine-gun fire. Finally, they rushed forward along with another company and took the north slope just in time to repulse a series of German counterattacks.

The last of these counterattacks was stopped singlehandedly by Gunnery Sergeant Charles Hoffman. He spotted a dozen enemy soldiers crawling through the bushes with several light machine guns. He charged down the slope with a yell, bayoneted two Germans and drove off the rest. Though badly wounded, he survived and received the Medal of Honor, America's highest award for bravery in combat. It was the first awarded to the Second Division.

Captain Crowther himself caught a bullet in the throat and was killed. His company, however, took Hill 142 as ordered. The cost was heavy. Ninety percent of the officers and 50% of the men were killed or wounded. It was a forecast of things to come.

At 3:45 P.M. Colonel Catlin, commander of the 6th Marine Regiment, looked through his binoculars to watch one of his battalions, under Major Benjamin Berry, move out into the wheat fields. Four-hundred yards beyond loomed the dark mass of Belleau Wood. "It was a moment fit to shake nerves of steel," wrote Catlin, "like entering a dark room filled with assassins."

Berry's men faced an almost impossible task. They crossed the field, the sun gleaming off their bayonets, the air sweet with the smell of trampled wheat. They were soon being cut down by Major Bischoff's veteran gunners. There were many acts of valor, but the Marines were pinned down until nightfall when they crawled back to the trench. With 60% casualties, including Major Berry, not one of them had reached the wood.

Colonel Catlin's second battalion, under Major Berton Sibley, fared somewhat better. Some were pinned by heavy fire, but the rest moved steadfastly forward and plunged into the wood.

Raising his binoculars again, Catlin grinned as the first wave of Marines disappeared among the trees. At that moment a bullet pierced his right lung and came out beneath his shoulder blade. Later, while recovering in Paris, Catlin told a visitor: "It's my own fault. I shouldn't have been so close to the front in a first-class war."

In the wood, Major Bischoff's machine guns covered every section with a gauntlet of fire. The Marines learned that the only effective tactic was to work around behind a nest and bomb it with hand grenades. Then they would rush forward and kill or capture the crew.

Bischoff's clever deployment made this deadly work. Every time Sibley's men took a machine-gun nest, they were pinned down by flanking fire from another.

One squad of Marines took a German nest only to get fired on by another nest. The Marines took cover behind some boulders, where they brought the surviving crew, then left one man behind to guard the

THE "DEVIL DOGS" OF BELLEAU WOOD
PROVIDED RICH POSTER MATERIAL AND
ATTRACTED A SURGE OF RECRUITS.
(NATIONAL ARCHIVES)

captured Germans. The rest of the squad sneaked around the flank of the second nest. They captured its whole crew. Meanwhile, the prisoners at the first nest had killed the guard and started firing at the second nest. The Marines bayoneted the crew of the second nest, then recaptured the first nest and killed its crew, too.

Between attacks Red Cross men on both sides helped the wounded. No one fired on them at first. Then some Marines spotted a German first aid team carrying a machine gun and some ammo boxes on a stretcher. "It looked like a wounded man with his legs drawn up," recalled an officer, "until a gust of wind flipped back the blanket covering the stretcher."

After that, it was hard on the medics and the wounded; it was hard on everyone. An unmailed letter, found later on the body of a German corporal and addressed to the corporal's father, told of the horror from the German perspective. "The Americans are savages," it said. "They kill everything that moves." This brutal, no-quarter fighting made the Germans call the Marines *Teufelhunden*—"Devil Dogs"—a nickname that sticks to this day.

The *New York Times* reported that on that first day the Marines charged forward crying "Remember the *Lusitania*." This seems an unlikely battle cry. No eyewitness accounts confirm it. Several accounts do mention a salty Marine sergeant yelling "Come on! Do you want to live forever?"

Darkness fell and the scene became a nightmare of yells, groans, cries for help, machine-gun bursts and rifle fire. By 9 P.M., Sibley had lost half his command, and the rest were held up at German strong points. He passed the word to dig in and wait for daybreak.

The commanding officer of the Marine brigade, Brigadier General James G. Harbord, reflected on the day's events. The Marines had suffered a staggering 1,100 casualties and captured only the southern lobe of the wood. The Germans still firmly held the northern and central parts. Yet his men had fought bravely and well, and at least they had a toehold.

It was apparent to Harbord that, as he later wrote, "More than Belleau Wood was at stake, more than standing between the invader and Paris. It was a struggle for psychological mastery. . . . The stage was small, but the audience was the world of 1918."

The German High Command had similar thoughts, and were paying close attention to the Marines. To abandon Belleau Wood would mean to give the Americans a "cheap success." International newspapers would headline that *one* brigade of Yanks was enough to stop the German attack. They felt that this might have serious consequences on the morale of the Central Powers and on the continuation of the war. They sent a crack division of Prussian Guard Infantry to reinforce the sector.

Thus both sides put more importance on the battle than the territory concerned deserved. Prestige was involved, a pivot on which great events can turn.

The next morning, June 8, Sibley's men renewed the advance. Losses were heavy. One company lost all its officers. General Harbord decided they had taken all the punishment they could stand. He ordered Sibley to pull out and take cover in a gully at the south edge of the wood.

The Army artillery took over now. The plan was to pulverize the enemy defenses with an intense barrage, then send in fresh Marine reserves to sweep clean the wood. On June 9, the artillery laid down 34,000 high-explosive shells. Most of the shells, however, had contact fuses that exploded when they hit the tops of the trees. The trenches beneath them were showered with branches and shrapnel, but the barrage caused relatively few casualties. When it was over, the Germans popped up behind their guns once more.

The Marines advanced. A private wrote: "We moved into the tree line. I saw blood-stained bodies everywhere, some missing an arm or leg. My knees felt weak and I wanted to sit down. . . . I guessed we were in Belleau Wood."

Three days of hard fighting gained some ground, but the enemy could not be dislodged from the wood. On June 13, the Germans counterattacked along the whole sector. In Belleau Wood, their main assault fell on Colonel Wise's battalion, the one that had first halted the Germans on the Paris highway 10 days earlier.

The battalion endured murderous attacks, but held on. Wise himself had a narrow escape while giving instructions to two of his officers. A shell burst overhead. It killed the officer on his right and incapacitated the one on his left. The shell fragments ripped through Wise's jacket but did not touch him.

That night, General Harbord sent another battalion, under Major Thomas Halcomb, to relieve Wise's hard-pressed men. It was unfortunate timing. As Halcomb's men started into the southern part of the wood, the Germans dropped 7,000 mustard gas bombs and many high explosive shells that also contained a vomiting gas.

Gas masks compounded the darkness and fog so that the men could not see anything. They stumbled through the blackness, bounding off trees and falling into shell holes.

THIS PAINTING BY MARINE CORPS ARTIST TOM LOVELL WAS AN
ATTEMPT TO CAPTURE THE HORROR OF COMBAT IN BELLEAU WOOD.
(U.S. MARINE CORPS)

Of Halcomb's 800 men, only 300 survivors drifted in to relieve
Colonel Wise. "I did not consider that they were sufficient to relieve me,"
reported Wise, "and remained in position."

On June 15, the U.S. Army took over the fight for a while. Harbord's
Marine brigade was relieved by the 7th Infantry Brigade of the 3rd U.S.

Division, which had not yet seen action. The Marine brigade had been cut down to less than half its original strength.

The next morning Colonel Wise reviewed his tattered battalion. He wrote: "It was enough to break your heart. I had left . . . on May 31 with 965 men and 26 officers. Now before me stood 350 men and six officers."

The French High Command was pleased and impressed with the performance of the 2nd Division (to which the Marines belonged). They weren't the only ones. On June 17, a copy of a German intelligence report (from a few days earlier) was captured. It contained this excerpt:

> *The American 2nd Division may be rated as a very good division. [In particular] the various attacks by both of the Marine regiments were carried out with vigor and regardless of losses. The effect of our firearms did not . . . check the advance of their infantry. The nerves of the Americans are still unshaken. . . . The personnel may be considered excellent. They are healthy, strong and physically well-developed men. The spirit of the American troops is fresh and one of careless confidence.*

Belleau Wood stood as the first testing ordeal between Germans and Americans on an otherwise insignificant wood patch. Without roads or rail lines, it was a springboard to nowhere, ground that neither side needed.

AISNE-MARNE AMERICAN CEMETERY, BELLEAU, FRANCE—
WITH MARBLE CROSSES.
(NATIONAL ARCHIVES)

The Germans were a bit foolish to let things happen the way they did. They placed the highest stakes on a local cockfight, and had taken on the wrong men. The Marine brigade was one of the most determined and aggressive units on the Western Front.

The Germans weren't licked yet. The 7th U.S. Infantry launched two assaults against Major Bischoff's men. Both were repulsed. On June 22, the Army gave Belleau Wood back to the Marines. A final assault on June 25 (led by Major Berry's old battalion) at last broke the enemy line. The Marines cleared the wood completely, bagging 500 German prisoners in the process.

The Marines had not won the war, but they had stopped the Germans in their tracks. For nearly four years the French army had been solely responsible for the Allies' right flank. At last, the French were not alone. The Yanks were in action.

✭ 15 ✭

TURNING THE TIDE

General Pershing knew how important it had been to help the French in their urgent hour of need. Yet, as the suspense eased, he grew impatient with General Foch, the Supreme Allied Commander. Although American troops were fighting together as units, Pershing felt it was time for an independent American Army under one command. Pershing urged Foch to give him an exclusively American sector of the front.

Foch preferred to attach American divisions piecemeal to large Allied army units commanded by French or British generals, but finally agreed. This plan, however, would have to be put on hold because the next German offensive came so fast.

Germany's generals had one last card to play. They planned a two-pronged attack, east and west of Rheims, hoping to surround and capture this key city, some 50 miles east of Paris. If successful, a drive on Paris might still be possible.

The German generals, it seemed, had failed to fully appreciate the mathematics of change on the Western Front. The numerical superiority of German manpower had made possible the slashing gains of early spring. By midsummer the constant flow of fresh, fit Americans had overcome that advantage and permanently reversed the whole situation.

This thought was a comfort to Allied commanders. Yet to the Allied soldiers the thought of another German offensive was as terrifying as ever. On July 15, 1918, the German stormtroopers struck hard.

The most notable American actions were along the south bank of the Marne River. At Château-Thierry the Germans made a ferocious assault against the 3rd U.S. Division, but the Yanks refused to yield.

At one point the 38th U.S. Infantry Regiment (part of the 3rd Division) was squeezed on three sides until it resembled a horseshoe. Despite the danger of encirclement, the men of the 38th held firm, inflicting three times as many casualties as they took. In one spot a dead American soldier was found with a rifle in one hand and a pistol in the other.

Surrounding him lay 12 dead Germans. For their steadfast defense, the 38th was given the nickname "Rock of the Marne."

East of Château-Thierry the 28th Pennsylvania National Guard Division also clung to every foot of ground. Four of its companies were surrounded, but continued to resist. When their ammunition ran out, they grappled with the enemy in hand-to-hand combat. The Pennsylvanians won praise from Pershing, who said "They fought like iron men." From this the 28th got its name. "The Iron Division."

Unable to penetrate the Allied line, the German offensive petered out on July 17. Along with it died Germany's last hope for victory. Now it was the German Army that was in peril.

On July 18 the Allies began their counterattack. By mid-August they had taken back all the territory the Germans had gained in their spring offensives. As summer ended, a total of 310,000 Americans had seen action, with 67,000 killed or wounded.

"Last night I witnessed a truly pitiful sight," one doughboy, Leo Cuthbertson, wrote home, "the burying of our boys. It makes one's blood run cold and increases a passionate desire to deal out misery to the enemy—and I believe before this war is over, he will have more misery than he bargained for."

If the Americans had come to France to fight for democracy, to this purpose they now added revenge and hatred. Watching their buddies get blown away, day after day, turned innocent youths into hardened killers. Gary Roberts of the 167th Infantry wrote home from a hospital:

> *I got two of the rascals and finished killing a wounded one with my bayonnet that might have gotten well had I not finished him. . . . I made the first two men holler 'mercy, comrade, mercy.' But how could I have mercy on such low-lifed rascals as they are. Why, I just couldn't kill them dead enough it didn't seem like. . . . The first one I got was for momma and the other one for myself.*

For the Allies, the danger had passed. The summer of 1918 had been the climax of the story of the Western Front. The grand finale was yet to come. For the soldiers on both sides, many frightful days still lay ahead.

By September, Pershing's dream of a self-sufficient American force of a million men had become a reality. He now sought to launch an offensive that was strictly American from beginning to end. Foch, a marshal by now, protested strongly. He still wanted to scatter American divisions among the French.

Pershing was furious. Even his divisional commanders were tired of having their troops thrown into areas they described as "meat grinders" while French units performed the mopping up operations. Perhaps Marshal Foch thought this was fair since the French army had suffered years of fighting, but Pershing saw it as no more than a means to get the most glory at the Americans' expense.

Pershing would no longer argue the issue. He threatened to withdraw all American units to their training areas until the dispute was resolved. Foch gave in. He knew Pershing was not bluffing.

For four years the Germans had held a bulge, around the city of St. Mihiel, that jutted like a dagger into the Allied line. Pershing drew up careful plans to flatten that bulge. On September 12, the doughboys of the 1st American Army attacked.

The operation went smoother than anyone had imagined. Pershing's timing could not have been better. The Germans, having caught wind of the plan, decided to pull out of the bulge. They were awkwardly caught in the middle of their withdrawal when the Americans attacked.

AMERICAN GUNNERS FIRING A FRENCH 75 AGAINST GERMAN TROOPS IN THE ST. MIHIEL SALIENT—1918. AFTER A LONG ARTILLERY BARRAGE, THE ATTACK WAS LAUNCHED.
(NATIONAL ARCHIVES)

Taken by surprise, many German strongholds surrendered. In one instance, a sergeant captured 300 prisoners with an empty pistol. By the next day, the American pincers had surrounded the German force in St. Mihiel. Some 15,000 Germans were captured, and many artillery pieces as well. It was September 13, Pershing's 58th birthday. He said it was the happiest one he had had for a long time.

There wasn't much time to celebrate. The Allies were planning a massive push along the entire front. Pershing had lest than two weeks to maneuver his army into position.

American casualties in the St. Mihiel offensive had been amazingly light. The operation was described as "a stroll." Indeed, it had been a picnic compared to what the doughboys were about to face in the Argonne Forest.

★ 16 ★

KNIGHTS OF THE AIR

An important factor in the success of the St. Mihiel operation was the superiority of Allied air power. An unprecedented force of 1,500 Allied planes gave General Pershing control of the skies. Although all the aircraft were of French or British make, many of the pilots were American.

This armada of combat airplanes would have been unimaginable four years earlier. When the war began, the total number of military aircraft in the world was only around 1,000.

Military thinkers had always understood the importance of knowing the enemy's whereabouts. By 1914 stationary gas-filled balloons were the primary craft for aerial reconnaissance. Raised and lowered from the ground by cables, they provided the observer with a stable platform from which to chart enemy artillery positions and troop movements.

When the war started, military planners were uncertain about the usefulness of airplanes. Planes at that time were very fragile and could carry only small pay loads. On the other hand, they were able to cover more area and had greater freedom of movement than balloons. They could also fly behind enemy lines.

As the armies marched to war in August 1914, airplanes flew ahead of them to gather information on the enemy. Aviation was a hazardous profession. Airplanes were made mostly of cloth and wood. They would sometimes rip apart in strong wind or when diving too fast. Their crude gasoline engines were unreliable and gave off choking fumes, including ether. Many early pilots crashed after being knocked unconscious by ether fumes.

At first there was a "chivalry" between the pilots of both sides. They saw each other as brother adventurers. Opposing pilots would pass each other with a friendly wave or salute.

That soon changed. Pilots, and especially observers (if it was a two-seater plane), began to fill their pockets with objects to fling at enemy aircraft. Chains and bricks were favorite weapons. But even after pistols replaced these, little damage was done.

When rifles started replacing pistols, aerial shooting became serious, although the difficulty of loading and aiming a rifle in the narrow confines of a cockpit kept the weapon from being more deadly. Shooting at a moving target through a maze of wires, struts and whirling propeller blades was tricky business. The firer often hit parts of his own plane.

Then one day a British observer took a machine gun into the air. The extra weight of the weapon made his plane unable to climb more than 3,500 feet. The observer spotted his prey, a German plane cruising at 5,000 feet. Firing the machine gun made a lot of noise and vibration, but had no effect on the enemy plane. Nonetheless, it was a significant milestone in aerial combat.

The rapid development of more powerful airplanes solved the problem of lifting a heavy machine gun into the air. There was still the problem of locating the gun where the pilot or observer could reach it, aim it and fire it—without hitting his own plane.

On many two-wing planes, the machine gun would be mounted on the top wing so that it could fire over the propeller. Firing it was easy enough, but reloading and in-flight repairs were impossible. The ideal was to have a machine gun directly in front of the cockpit. This way the pilot could easily reach the weapon. Aiming would just be a matter of pointing his plane toward the enemy.

The French led the way by attaching a metal wedge to the propeller, which deflected the bullets that would otherwise shoot the blades off. At first this seemed a promising solution, but it was found the striking bullets created too much stress on the propeller blades. The French air service abandoned the invention.

The big breakthrough came in the spring of 1915 when Germany developed a mechanism that synchronized the spin of the propeller with the stream of bullets. A device was hooked up to the machine gun so that it would not fire whenever the blade was in the way. By the end of May, Germany's new forward-firing guns were shooting Allied planes out of the sky.

The synchronization device gave German pilots a distinct advantage in aerial combat. It was a year before the Allies developed their own mechanism for forward-firing.

To the soldiers wallowing in the mud below, battles between airplanes, called dogfights, were gripping spectacles that broke the monotony of trench life. In a war where millions of men had become faceless numbers to be manipulated by generals, the solo nature of the dogfights had tremendous romantic appeal.

Combat pilots became bigger-than-life heroes. These airborne warriors were a special breed of men, fighting their own individual battles high above the mud. The media depicted them as modern-day knights, jousting for the skies.

An American pilot named Henry Palmer wrote to his brother later in the war: "It is great sport, and all I ask is that I take a few [Germans] down with me." (Sadly, Palmer died in a French hospital of pneumonia.)

Combat aviation may have been more glamorous than being in the infantry, but it was no less deadly. In a dogfight the slightest mistake could cost the pilot his life. The life expectancy of a combat pilot was only 40 to 60 hours of flight time.

For the aviator, death usually came in two of its most terrible forms—by fire or falling from a great height. There were no parachutes for pilots yet, but many preferred to leap from their flaming planes rather than burn to death in their cockpits. No wonder that pilots called their machines "flying coffins." Yet aviators agreed that ascending, well-groomed and well-fed, to be killed in an airplane was better than going over-the-top from some filthy trench, to be mashed up in No-Man's-Land amid rotting corpses.

On April 18, 1916, seven Americans formed a fighter plane squadron (*escadrille* in French) that was to become one of the most famous and romanticized of all air units. They called themselves the *Escadrille Americaine*. Later they changed the name to *Escadrille Lafayette* in honor of the French general and hero of the American Revolution.

France provided the squadron with planes and other necessary equipment. All the pilots were American volunteers serving under the French flag. Needless to say, the *Escadrille Lafayette* added to the growing tension between Germany and the supposedly neutral United States.

In a short time the squadron captured America's heart. On May 18, 1916, it downed its first enemy aircraft. Soon, other Americans already serving in France were transferred to the *Escadrille Lafayette*. Raoul Lufbery, who had been among the Americans who enlisted as infantrymen in the French Foreign Legion in 1914, reported for duty on May 24, 1916.

Lufbery had been a well-known aviator before the war. Now he was to become the most skillful and successful fighter pilot of the *Escadrille*

Lafayette. In August, Lufbery became America's first ace. (To become an ace, a pilot needed to have five confirmed downings of enemy aircraft.)

Lufbery became a hero. French and American newspapers were full of his picture and stories of his airborne exploits. He received bundles of fan mail from admirers. Children were named after him.

Lufbery was officially credited with 17 kills. No one will know for sure how many enemy aircraft he knocked out since many went down behind German lines, without witnesses, and were not counted. The French and American nations mourned after Major Raoul Lufbery was killed in a dogfight on May 19, 1918.

At the time of Lufbery's death, the United States had been in the war for over a year but was just forming its own independent air service. Three months earlier, the *Escadrille Lafayette* had been disbanded. Its gallant pilots had earned the squadron 57 confirmed victories. Nine of the pilots had been killed in action. (Of the original seven men who formed the squadron, only one survived the war unscathed.)

In the United States, aircraft production was slow to get off the ground. In fact, the war ended before any American planes were sent to France. All the aircraft in the new United States Air Service were French-built, but the planes now had American insignia and markings.

The first American combat air unit was the 95th Aero Squadron. The planes the French had sent to the unit had no machine guns. Undaunted by the lack of weapons, the bold American aviators flew unarmed reconnaissance missions over hostile territory.

After several weeks, the Allies started to criticize the Americans. Allied Command had received reports of aerial engagements by the squadron, with one American pilot lost but so far no enemy planes shot down by the 95th.

The American squadron commander returned a report saying that the 95th would be most happy to shoot down enemy planes if the Allied command would see fit to supply it with machine guns. After this report, the squadron was immediately pulled from the line and fitted with machine guns.

No pilot did more to enhance the reputation of the 95th than Eddie Rickenbacker. A world-famous race car driver and, for a time, General Pershing's personal chauffeur, Rickenbacker put his skill and talent into flying. With 26 confirmed kills to his credit, Captain Rickenbacker was America's leading ace of the First World War.

LEADING AMERICAN ACE OF THE AIR WAR—
CAPTAIN EDDIE RICKENBACKER.
(LIBRARY OF CONGRESS)

No American pilot had more of a mystique than Second Lieutenant Frank "Balloon Buster" Luke of the U.S. 27th Aero Squadron. An audacious and talented pilot, Luke became, in less than three weeks' time, America's second greatest ace. A loner, Luke preferred to perform missions on his own. Because his reckless behavior in the air made him dangerous to fly with, Luke's commander gave him permission to operate alone.

One important function of fighter planes was to shoot down enemy observation balloons. Because of antiaircraft fire from the ground and enemy fighters assigned to protect these observers, "balloon busting" was a treacherous task. When Luke was told that it was the most difficult and dangerous job a pilot could undertake, he decided to be the best.

Luke's war on balloons began on September 12, 1918, when he sent one down in flames. He shot down two balloons on the 14th, three more on the 15th and another three on the 16th. On September 18, he shot down two balloons and three enemy fighters. As a reward Luke was granted leave in Paris, but he came back early. On September 26, he downed a German plane, and another balloon on the 27th.

Luke was an excellent pilot, but not the most disciplined soldier. When ordered to do something, he was often defiant, as well as repeatedly

AWOL, or absent without leave. On September 29 Lieutenant Frank Luke was placed under arrest and, at the same time, awarded the Distinguished Service Cross for valor.

Luke was grounded, but managed to take off in his plane before he could be apprehended. As he flew over the American trenches, he dropped a note to the doughboys below that read: "Watch for three Hun balloons on the Meuse."

American observers looked on as three enemy balloons became earthbound fireballs. While downing his third victim, antiaircraft shrapnel ripped into Luke's plane. Unable to gain altitude, Luke was forced to crash-land in a nearby meadow behind enemy lines.

Lucky as ever, Luke climbed out of his cockpit without a scratch. He was, however, surrounded by German soldiers. They shouted at him to surrender, but Frank Luke refused. He stood defiantly in the meadow, shooting his pistol at them until he was killed.

More than 650 American aviators saw action during the war. Although they lost 316 aircraft to the enemy, they took down 927 German airplanes and balloons—an impressive kill ratio of almost three-to-one.

By mid-September 1918, the Allies had achieved supremacy in the air. Yet the soldiers on the ground still had a long way to go. For General Pershing and the doughboys, the biggest test and worst ordeal now faced them in the Argonne Forest.

★ 17 ★

INTO THE ARGONNE

After the mop-up at St. Mihiel, only 12 days remained for General Pershing to get his forces on the starting line for the huge, frontwide Allied push to begin September 26. American troops would take part all along the line. The U.S. 91st Division would fight with the Belgian army in the Ypres sector under the command of King Albert. Two more U.S. divisions would be part of a huge British effort on the Somme and another two (including the 2nd Division) would participate under the French army.

The big show for Pershing and the newly-formed 1st American Army would be in the Meuse-Argonne region, a few miles north of Verdun. The jump-off line extended 24 miles from the Meuse River on the right across to and through the Argonne Forest on the left.

The movement of tremendous amounts of men and equipment had to be made in secrecy. This meant shifting more than 800,000 troops, all under the cover of darkness so as not to be detected. Marshal Foch doubted that the Americans would be able to pull it off.

There were only three main roads, all with deep ruts. Down these mud roads, a seemingly endless convoy of French trucks, driven by sleepy-eyed Vietnamese, crawled along by night—without lights. The cramped Americans they carried were tormented by cold, rain, mosquitos and exhaust fumes. The men were so closely packed they could not sleep.

Despite the difficulties, the Americans kept on schedule. The American Army even managed to get in place a day before the earliest date that Foch thought possible. Evidence suggests that the Germans were not aware of the move.

Yet Pershing was worried. In order to meet Foch's deadline, he had put untried divisions on the primary points of attack. So limited was the experience of these green troops that they could hardly be classified as soldiers. Winston Churchill would later write that the Americans were "half trained, half organized, with only their courage, their numbers and their magnificent youth behind their weapons."

AMERICAN TROOPS BOARDING TRUCKS BOUND FOR THE
ARGONNE BATTLEFRONT.
(NATIONAL ARCHIVES)

Of the nine divisions taking part in the opening assault, only two had combat experience (one was the veteran 28th "Iron" Division). Along this Argonne section was the 77th Division, made up of draftees from New York City. It was an odd decision to send a division of inner-city men into dense forest.

Each doughboy carried 200 rounds of ammunition, two cans of corned beef, six boxes of hardtack (Army biscuits) and a one-quart canteen. Many of the novice troops put wine in their canteens instead of water. They had no veterans around to warn them that in the heat of battle wine was likely to turn a man's stomach as well as increase his dehydration. Later, men who should have been busy knocking out Germans would be busy throwing up.

On September 25, the eve of battle, the Americans waited silently in their positions. It rained softly. According to one infantry private from Mississippi, it was "as though the heavens were weeping over the sacrifice of so many lives that was so soon to be made."

The Americans could not have faced a more challenging obstacle. For hundreds of years, the Meuse-Argonne region had stood as a natural barrier between French kings and German princes. It was a tangle of ravines, woods, dominating heights and rock-bound citadels. It was ideal for defense.

For four years, the Germans had been improving what nature started. They built a thick belt of defensive earthworks strengthened by wire, steel and concrete. Its three main trench lines—named after three fabled witches of a Wagnerian opera—were deep and elaborate. The German trenches even had wooden beds and electric lights.

It was Belleau Wood all over again, but on a much larger scale. One American general said that it made the Virginia forest where Grant and Lee fought the battle of the Wilderness look like a park. Pershing, however, commanded 12 times as many troops as Grant did at that battle in 1864, used 10 times as many cannon and had more ammunition than the Union Army used during the whole Civil War.

Following a three-hour bombardment by 2,700 guns, at 5:30 A.M. on September 26, 1918, the Americans began their assault. Despite an eight-to-one numerical superiority, the advance began to bog down after

AMMUNITION AND SUPPLIES MOVE FORWARD, WHILE CAISSONS AND AMBULANCES STREAM BACK FROM THE ARGONNE BATTLEFRONT.
(NATIONAL ARCHIVES)

about a mile. Evening fell with the troops five miles short of the first day's target. The offensive turned into stagnation the second day, and as September ended the advance ground to a halt. By this time, however, more veteran divisions were available to hurl into the attack.

Foot by foot the attack continued. Through rain and sleet, the soldiers inched their way up the treacherous landscape under constant enemy fire. They crawled through the clinging wire on whose rusty barbs pieces of cloth and flesh would remain. They fell into pits and were impaled on spikes that the Germans had cleverly set up for that purpose.

Keeping the troops supplied was also becoming a problem. As the soldiers advanced past the Germans' first line of defense, they left behind them a four-year-old No-Man's-Land (the same field the battle of Verdun had been fought on). It was a veritable lunar landscape over which serviceable roads would have to be built before supplies could be brought up.

Along with the mud and entanglements, there were mine craters 100 feet wide and 40 feet deep. One soldier described them as "wounds where the very bowels of the earth had been torn out . . . Imagine the ocean at its roughest and then imagine it instantly turned to clay." The time it took to reestablish supply lines gave the Germans the chance to reinforce the sector with more troops.

Meanwhile, the Manhattan men of the 77th Division were learning that the Argonne was a long way from Central Park. Yet they pressed on through the forest, meeting fierce resistance every step of the way. Leading the way was the 1st Battalion of the 308th Infantry Regiment, commanded by Major Charles Wittlesey.

On October 1 the battalion made its way into a small valley with steep, wooded banks, about a half-mile in front of the rest of the division. Sensing a trap, Wittlesey ordered his men back across the brook. He was too late. As the men crossed an old footbridge, German machine guns opened up. The battalion was trapped in the valley.

One of Wittlesey's messengers made it to the rear to request assistance. The 307th Regiment was sent, but only one company made it through. The rest were lost in the dark forest or driven off by enemy fire. By morning (October 2) Wittlesey and over 600 men were completely surrounded.

Throughout the day German mortars, grenades and snipers took their toll. Totally isolated, there was no way for divisional headquarters to contact the 1st Battalion. Wittlesey, however, had a few homing

AMERICAN SOLDIERS FACE AN ENEMY BARRAGE IN THE ARGONNE.
(NATIONAL ARCHIVES)

pigeons that he could send to let them know he and his men had not surrendered.

The next day (October 3) was spent fending off German assaults. By noon, the last of the food had been eaten. The only source of water, a spring, had a German machine gun trained on it. There were many wounded but there was no medical officer. All the bandages had been used up.

By the morning of October 4, less than 500 men were still alive. Unable to get infantry in to relieve the 1st Battalion, the 77th Division Command decided to saturate the German positions with artillery fire. But the American artillery, which had only an approximate idea of the battalion's position, dropped its shells on Wittlesey's men.

Wittlesey released his last homing bird, his only hope. The slate-colored carrier pigeon was named Cher Ami. (*Cher ami* is a common French opening for a personal letter and means "dear friend.") The pigeon instinctively flew toward the American lines.

Along the way a bullet crashed into Cher Ami's head, tearing out its left eye. Then flaming shrapnel tore into its chest and fractured its breastbone. A third hit ripped away its lower right leg. Yet, miraculously, the pigeon kept flying. Wittlesey's message was still there, hanging from the torn ligaments of Cher Ami's remaining leg. The message finally reached the American artillery. It read: "For heaven's sake, stop it."

The shelling had lasted over an hour and caused at least 30 casualties. It also tore away underbrush that hid the doughboys from enemy snipers. By October 6 only 275 men were left. The Germans urged Wittlesey and his men to surrender. They refused.

Rain at least provided drinking water. The men resorted to eating plant roots and even the bird seed left by the pigeon handler. Allied aircraft dropped food and other supplies, but most of it landed on the German side. German snipers laid out the food packages, killing any American who reached for the bait.

On October 7, weak from hunger and exposure to the cold, and with almost no ammunition left, the men settled into another hopeless night. Then, a little past 7 P.M., three companies of the 307th Infantry finally cut their way through.

On October 8, the 194 survivors of what became known as the "Lost Battalion" left the valley. On that same day in another part of the forest, Alvin C. York in just 15 minutes made his reputation as the most famous American hero of World War I.

York was part of a 16-man patrol sent to knock out several enemy machine-gun nests holding a wooded slope. The patrol quietly slipped behind the German lines. In a small clearing it surprised a German battalion commander and a group of soldiers. Thinking the patrol was part of a large force of Americans, the Germans threw up their hands in surrender.

The German soldiers on the next rise realized the American force was small and opened fire. Six men of the American squad were immediately killed and three more wounded, including the officer in charge.

The captured Germans lay down on the ground while the remaining seven men of the patrol took cover behind some trees. The Germans, now shooting from two sides, created a crossfire, which hit not only the Americans, but also those Germans who had already surrendered and their own troops firing from the opposite side.

The American patrol returned fire and killed several Germans. York then took command of the patrol. He ordered them to watch the prisoners while he moved out to attack the other enemy positions. York had grown up in the mountains of Tennessee hunting small game and was a crack shot. He now put his marksmanship to work.

One by one York shot the Germans in the first position with his rifle. Then another group charged him from the side with bayonets. Instinctively York pulled out his Colt .45 automatic pistol and aimed. He intentionally fired at the men in the rear of the oncoming squad so that the ones in front would keep charging. He worked his shots forward until he hit the last man.

In all, York took out 17 German soldiers with exactly 17 shots. York and the rest of the patrol then marched the prisoners back to the American lines. Along the way the major they had captured ordered more Germans to surrender. The seven Americans got back safely with their three wounded comrades and 132 German prisoners. York was awarded the Congressional Medal of Honor.

There were many heroes of the Argonne, but Alvin York was the most famous and popular. Perhaps this was because he symbolized America's citizen soldiers. York was a conscientious objector—that is, he thought all war was bad and had said that fighting in one was against his religious

AMERICAN INFANTRY OF THE 1ST ARMY TAKE A REST AFTER CAPTURING TERRITORY FROM THE GERMANS IN THE BATTLE-SCARRED ARGONNE FOREST.
(NATIONAL ARCHIVES)

beliefs. When he was drafted, he entered the Army only after "a lot of prayer and soul searching."

York understood duty to his country. He did what he had to do. He became a legend, but had no pride in what he had done.

The day after the fight, he wrote in his journal: "I didn't want to kill a whole heap of Germans, I didn't hate them, but I done it just the same." In World War II, York would serve his country again as a counselor for young men who wished to be declared conscientious objectors.

On October 10 the Americans drove the last Germans from the Argonne. The British and French drives farther north had cracked key German defensive lines. It was becoming clear to the Germans that the war was lost. Germany's diplomats began to probe for peace.

☆ 18 ☆

THE ELEVENTH HOUR

The German army continued to give ground on the Western Front throughout October 1918. Yet as measured on the map of Europe, Germany's peril was not obvious. In the East, German troops occupied a vast stretch of the Russian empire from the Baltic Sea to the Black Sea. In the West, Germany still had most of Belgium as well as troops firmly entrenched on French soil.

The Allies were anticipating a long, drawn-out fight. The German army was battered and bloody, but not broken. It would surely die hard. Few Allied military or political leaders believed the war would end before mid-1919.

The Germans, however, had lost hope for the future. They knew the French and British were exhausted, but fresh American soldiers were landing in France at the rate of 10,000 men every 24 hours. It would only be a matter of time until the United States' enormous resources, production and manpower overwhelmed Germany.

In early October Berlin began sending notes to President Wilson, from whom the Germans thought they could get the best arrangement for peace. Although Wilson favored some leniency toward Germany, he was not in a position to make decisions without consulting France and Britain.

Wilson's main concern was that Germany become a democracy. "I have no quarrel with the German people," he would say. Then on October 10, 1918, a U-boat sank a British passenger ferry in the English Channel. Hundreds perished, including women, children and some Americans.

Public outrage, and his own anger, forced Wilson to take a firmer stand. He replied to Berlin that it would be left up to the Allied military leaders to determine the conditions for an armistice. The Allied generals took Germany's peace initiative as a sign of weakness. They resolved to push harder than ever against the German army.

Although the Allies now realized that the end of the war was near, the generals gave orders not to inform the soldiers at the front. They did not want the effort of the troops to slacken while the two sides negotiated. Pershing sent a strong order to his division commanders:

> *Now that Germany and the Central Powers are losing, they are begging for an armistice. Their request is an acknowledgement of weakness and clearly means that the Allies are winning the war. That is the best of reasons for our pushing the war more vigorously at this moment. . . . We must strike harder than ever. . . . There can be no conclusion to this war until Germany is brought to her knees.*

Meanwhile the Allied armies were making much progress on other fronts. On September 29, 1918, Bulgaria surrendered. The crumbling Ottoman Empire signed an armistice on October 30 as did Austria-Hungary on November 3.

On November 10, Germany's last monarch gave up his throne, his crown and his country. Kaiser Wilhelm II abdicated and fled to Holland. There he puttered, gardened and spoke endless "if onlys" until his death in 1941.

At 5 A.M. on November 11, 1918, Germany signed an armistice with the Allies. Yet the truce did not go into effect that moment. It had been decided by the Allied representatives that, for the sake of historical drama, the war would not end until precisely 11 A.M.—that is, the eleventh hour of the eleventh day of the eleventh month.

This six-hour delay for the sake of a good newspaper headline was an unpardonable gesture. Across the front it was taken by many commanders as a signal for a final bloodbath.

Artillery units everywhere fired frantically, usually without even aiming. Both sides seemed to be trying to shoot every last shell so that none would be left over.

Many American infantry units were ordered to advance right up to 11 A.M. "We thought it was a joke," wrote Lieutenant Harry C. Rennagel of the U.S. 101st Infantry Regiment. It was no joke. It was the final convulsion of the most horrific and costly war in history.

Lieutenant Rennagel had left the hospital the day before and arrived at his outfit at 10 A.M. on November 11. He was joking and laughing with his men, "waiting for the gong to ring when orders came to go over-the-top." He and his men moved out as ordered, at 25 minutes to 11. They advanced as slowly and as cautiously as they could.

At 10:55 A.M. Lieutenant Rennagel heard gunfire. "I hurried over and there lay five of my best men." He knelt beside one of the young men who had a hole near his heart.

SHOUTS OF JOY AND TOSSED HELMETS ARE THE REACTION,
AFTER SOLDIER READS TERMS OF ARMISTICE TO HIS FRIENDS.
(NATIONAL ARCHIVES)

"Lieutenant," said the fatally injured soldier, "I'm going fast. Don't say I'll get better, you know different and this is a pretty unhappy time for me. You know we all expected things to cease today, so I wrote my girl. We were to be married when I returned, and [I told her and] my folks that I was safe and well and about my plans. And now—by some order—I am not going home."

"I looked away," said Lieutenant Rennagel, "and when I looked back—he had gone . . . I can honestly tell you I cried and so did the rest."

Suddenly, across the entire Western Front, everything stopped. Mouths wide open, soldiers stared into No-Man's-Land, dumbstruck by the wonderful quiet that now reigned.

A few minutes later, men began to cry, laugh, shake hands, slap each other on the back and then to cheer wildly. For the first time, men stood up straight in their foxholes. They walked in the open with nothing to fear. They built campfires for the first time. They took off their boots, dried their socks and warmed their chilled fingers.

Within minutes Yanks and Germans got together in the middle ground. Most left their rifles in the trenches. Active bartering sprang up. Dough-boys gave the Germans cigarettes, food rations and soap in exchange for belt buckles, bayonets and even a few Iron Crosses (German army medals).

Most of the fighting men were too dazed to think much about the future. Relief and joy were all they felt. "No more bombs," said one Yank, "no more mangled, bleeding bodies, no more exposure to terrifying shell fire in the rain and cold and mud! It will be difficult to adjust the mind to the new state of things."

When the eleventh hour struck, it was only 6 A.M. in Washington and New York. There were no radios to spread the news. Yet within hours, a national "yahoo!" had started along the East Coast and spread westward.

In towns and cities throughout France and Britain, people took to the streets in celebration. The crowds became drunk with excitement. In London people smashed shop windows and overturned vehicles. In the end, the London police had to clear the streets and put a few rowdies in jail.

ARMISTICE CELEBRATION IN ALSACE-LORRAINE, 1918.
(NATIONAL ARCHIVES)

Berlin was even more rowdy, but for another reason. Defeat had caused civil strife and violence to break out. Returning soldiers were horrified to find barricades in the streets of the German capital. They heard the crack of rifle fire and felt the concussion of grenades. Some soldiers had survived the long war only to be shot down in their own city by fellow citizens.

✳ 19 ✳

THE ROAD HOME

THE END OF "THE WAR TO END WAR," CELEBRATED IN
PHILADELPHIA—NOVEMBER 11, 1918
(NATIONAL ARCHIVES)

By the morning of November 12, 1918, the frenzy of the previous day was beginning to settle. As the doughboys began to grasp the reality of the armistice, their thoughts turned to how soon they could go home. Unhappily, demobilizing the American Expeditionary Force would be a large and complex task.

British ships and French railroads had been used to help put the American Army in the field. Now they were needed to get the Army out of it. The French and British, however, had their own forces to bring home. The Americans would have to wait.

The long wait was hard on the doughboys. Men became irritable. Relations with the locals and each other became strained.

Overseas mail service, which was bad during the war, did not improve in the first months of peace. Food service got even worse. Weary American troops were herded into camps and there forgotten. Most camps were seas of half-frozen mud where the men had to live in tents through the dead of winter. There was almost no fuel to be had and too few blankets.

From these hardships, along with the boredom, grew much bitterness and disillusion among the American troops. Yet their neglect was not deliberate. The AEF had grown too large too quickly. The problem of administration had simply overwhelmed the Army's leaders. Before things got better for the men, there would be one more misery.

Throughout the fall of 1918, a virulent influenza epidemic had raged in the United States. Half-a-million Americans, four times the number killed overseas during the war, would die from the flu. Some of the last doughboys to arrive in France were already infected.

The disease spread through the crowded camps faster than bad news. The epidemic increased throughout the AEF by 10,000 cases per week. At one camp the men died at a rate of 250 per day.

Many American units soon found out that they were not going home at all. Rather, they would be a part of the Allied force assigned to occupy the western part of Germany, called the Rhineland. Many complained that they had joined the Army to fight, not to be policemen.

Getting to Germany was not easy. Roads had to be built over No-Man's-Land. Beyond that, rail service was almost nonexistent. Demolition devices had to be removed from bridges and highways.

The weeks after the armistice brought long and punishing marches for the doughboys, in worn-out shoes, stained red from the soldiers' raw and bleeding feet. It was mid-December by the time the occupying American troops reached the German frontier.

The months following the armistice would also be sour ones for the American soldiers stationed in Russia. Back in March 1918, the Germans had forced the Soviet government into signing the harsh treaty of Brest–Litovsk. Under the terms of the treaty, Russia yielded a third of her population, a third of her farmland, half of her industry and 90% of her coal mines.

But throughout the summer the German army had continued to push deep into Russian territory. In August the Allies began sending troops into Russia, supposedly to reestablish an Eastern Front.

That month 7,000 U.S. soldiers were sent to the Pacific port of Vladivostok in Siberia to protect 800,000 tons of rusting Allied equipment that had been shipped to help the Russian army back when it was still fighting the Germans. American troops were also sent to Russia's arctic ports of Archangel and Murmansk, supposedly to prevent the Germans from establishing submarine bases there.

Yet in the clashes that followed, it was not the German army that the Allies were fighting. It was the communist-led, Soviet Red Army. Some Allied leaders secretly wanted the Allied forces in Russia to be used to oppose the Soviet government and help the anti-communist "White" Russians regain power. This fact became more obvious after Germany's surrender ended the military reasons for occupying northern Russia.

The confused American troops had no idea why they were there. They thought that they were headed for the trenches of France. Their first letters home began: "Guess where I am."

In the battle of Armistice Day (November 11, 1918) 28 U.S. soldiers were killed fighting communist troops. As the furious and merciless Russian Civil War raged between Whites and Reds, doughboys were sometimes caught in the middle. In all, some 200 Americans died in Russia.

In August 1919, the American Archangel force officially ended its operation and withdrew. An American lieutenant wrote: "Not a soldier knew, no not even vaguely, why he had fought, or why he was going now, or why his comrades were left behind, beneath the wooden crosses." The American expedition in Siberia finally came to an end on April Fools' Day, 1920.

When the summer of 1919 ended, all but five American divisions had been sent home. General Pershing himself sailed in September. The last 2,000 American troops left Europe in 1923. They brought home with them the last of some 1,200 German war brides who married doughboys during the occupation.

✫ 20 ✫

RECKONING

Although most of the struggle of 1914–18 took place in Europe, it does deserve to be called a World War. Fighting took place on three continents and three oceans. On all six continents there were countries at war. A total of 28 countries (with a combined population of 1.4 billion people) were involved by the end of the war.

The war began with five Allied countries pitted against two for the Central Powers. Within a year, the Ottoman Empire and Bulgaria entered the war. Against these four enemies the number of Allies grew to 24 by war's end. Five more countries broke off diplomatic relations with Germany. Only 16 countries, making up one-sixteenth of the world population, remained neutral.

Even tiny San Marino, a country only 38 square miles in size, joined the Allies and sent 300 men to fight in the Italian army. Although the majority of countries that eventually joined the Allies made only a token contribution to the war effort, the awakening of the world against the Central Powers had a considerable moral effect.

With the war over, the statisticians set about the task of tallying the cost of the war, in lives and money. The staggering figures they came up with broke every record in history to that time.

The direct monetary cost of the war was something like $186,000,000,000, in 1918 dollars—an extraordinary sum, even in today's dollars. To this must be added the indirect cost of the war. When the loss of production, shipping, property and the economic value of the people killed are figured in, the total cost of the war was at least a third of a trillion dollars.

For a time, international trade would be disrupted by the shortage of ships caused by the war. Five-thousand Allied ships were sunk by U-boats. Another 700 were the victims of mines, airplanes and surface raiders.

U-boat sinkings (in tons):
1914–310,000
1915–1,301,000
1916–2,322,000
1917–6,270,000
1918–2,659,000

Unlike economically ruined Europe, the U.S. economy emerged stronger than it had been before the war. Yet the war directly cost the United States about $24 billion. In addition, by war's end, America had loaned $10 billion to various countries.

Most important was the loss of life. There was hardly a family in France, Germany and Britain that did not lose a loved one. Newspaper items like this one from Britain were typical: "Private Thomas Pestorisk . . . has been so badly wounded that he has been invalided out of the service. . . . He is the youngest of nine brothers who joined the Army and he has lost eight brothers in the war."

A SHATTERED CHURCH IN THE RUINS OF NEUVILLY, CLOSE TO
THE ARGONNE FOREST, SERVED AS A HOSPITAL FOR THE
WOUNDED AS THE BATTLE WAS WAGED.
(NATIONAL ARCHIVES)

One historian suggests that the machine gun was the great killer of World War I. A relatively new weapon, military planners failed to realize the machine gun's potential as a defensive weapon. It greatly multiplied the killing power of the soldier who operated it. One squeeze of the trigger could mow down whole ranks of men.

Another historian suggests that artillery was the great killer. Cannon had been improved much in the previous half-century. They became death-dealing, rapid-fire monsters capable of delivering torrents of explosive shells. At Verdun, for example, 40 million shells were fired over a six-month period. (All the artillery rounds fired by the Union Army during all four years of the Civil War totaled only about five million.)

Yet most historians agree that the great killer of World War I was the arrogance, stupidity and stubbornness of the generals and politicians on both sides. They stripped their nations of manpower and led them into an upward spiral of mass slaughter. As the bloodbath dragged on year after year, the generals and politicians made cold-blooded calculations of how long they could continue to fight before the entire manhood of their nations was wiped out.

Yet what kept the soldiers and the civilian masses going was the hope that their horrible suffering was not in vain. They clung to the belief that this war would be the last one. Some called it Armageddon—the final contest between good and evil referred to in the Bible. The most widespread motto of the war sought to justify the struggle by calling it "the war to end war."

Whatever the reasons for continuing the war, continue it did. The casualty rates were staggering. For example, the British army lost an average of 19,000 soldiers each month in 1915, 44,000 soldiers per month in 1916, 56,000 per month in 1917 and a ghastly 75,000 per month in 1918.

Warfare had never been fought on such a scale. The major battles often engaged over a million men between both sides. Compare that to, say, the American Revolution, which rarely saw more than 10,000 men engaged. In 1814 the British captured Washington, D.C. with only 3,500 men.

In all, over 60 million men were pressed into military service. Russia mobilized the most men, followed by Germany, the British empire, then France.

Yet France mobilized the highest percentage of its population and the French army suffered the highest percentage of casualties. One out of every five French citizens was inducted into the armed forces. Over 90% of France's able-bodied males of military age served in the army, of which more than 70% were casualties.

No one will ever know how many lives were lost in the war. It has been estimated that 11,000,000 soldiers died. About double that number were wounded, many incapacitated for life. The war was also responsible, directly or indirectly, for the death of perhaps 10,000,000 civilians.

One of the grimmest scenes of modern history took place in what is now eastern Turkey, where a large number of Christian Armenians lived. Isolated cases of collaboration between local Armenians and Russian forces had convinced the government of the Ottoman Turks that the whole Armenian population was disloyal. The Turks decided to massacre them with a calculated program of systematic genocide. One-and-a-half-million Armenians perished in this little known holocaust.

The war decimated a generation of Europe's youth. By comparison, the loss of American life seems slight. Yet in only five months of active fighting, some 37,926 doughboys were killed in action. Another 13,628 died of wounds received in action. Disease claimed the lives of 23,853 men overseas and 38,815 men in the United States. Other causes brought the U.S. Army's total dead to 120,144.

In addition, 198,059 American soldiers were wounded. Of these, 700 men had hands or feet amputated, 600 had lost arms and 1,700 went home missing a leg or two. Many were blinded by gas.

To put this human price tag in perspective, consider the cost of the American Revolution. Between 1775 and 1783, 6,800 American soldiers were killed. More men died in a week's fighting in the Argonne Forest.

For the men who fought in the trenches their lives would never be the same. Many had disfiguring wounds. Prolonged exposure to the constant dampness gave some men a rasping cough that they would never lose. Others found their hands would occasionally shake uncontrollably.

Many veterans suffered from psychological or nervous disorders, ranging from nightmares and bed-wetting to depression and suicide. There were shell-shocked victims, men whose minds snapped under the strain of fear from constant bombardment. Some of these men kept their faces constantly covered with their hands to protect themselves from red-hot shell splinters, even though the splinters had long since stopped flying.

Whatever their problems, the doughboys were glad to be home. A returning soldier, elated to see the Statue of Liberty as his troopship at last entered New York harbor, yelled at the monument: "Old girl, if you ever want to look me in the face again, you'll have to turn around on your pedestal."

☆ 21 ☆

THE WAR TO END WAR

The armistice had ended the fighting, but not the war. World War I would not be over until a peace treaty was signed. In January 1919, thousands of Allied delegates went to Versailles, France, where a peace conference was held. German delegates were not invited.

In fact, as far as the Allies were concerned, they were still at war. The half- starved German population would stay that way, for the Allies refused to lift the naval blockade. This cruel and inhumane decision resulted in a terrible famine in Germany. German children starved to death while diplomats in Versailles dickered for months over the terms of the treaty.

President Wilson sailed for Europe in December 1918. He was the first president to leave the country while in office. Wherever he went, the populace gave him a tumultuous reception. Many people throughout the continent believed that their hopes for a better world were in Wilson's hands.

The President's proposal for a democratic and progressive world peace was called the "Fourteen Points." They included plans for arms reduction, abolition of secret treaties, rights for colonial subjects, a halt to interference in Russian affairs and self-determination of peoples based on ethnic boundaries, not political ones.

The Allies were not overly enthusiastic about the Fourteen Points. Each Allied government found a few provisions it did not like. Britain, for example, opposed the point that called for freedom of the seas.

The Allies had won the war and wanted to dictate their own terms and redraw the map of Europe as they saw fit. Allied representatives at Versailles were becoming very tired of Wilson's high ideals. The venerable Georges Clemenceau, the French premier and chairman of the peace conference, said: "Wilson bores me with his Fourteen Points. Why, God Almighty only had ten."

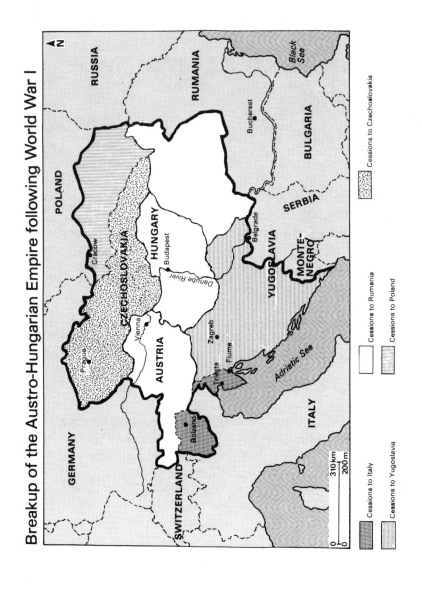

Breakup of the Austro-Hungarian Empire following World War I

"COUNCIL OF FOUR" AT THE PEACE CONFERENCE: PRESIDENT
WOODROW WILSON, PREMIER CLEMENCEAU, PREMIER ORLANDO,
AND PRIME MINISTER LLOYD GEORGE—MAY 27, 1919.
(LIBRARY OF CONGRESS)

Wilson's 14th point called for the establishment of a League of Nations. He believed that a strong international coalition was needed to ensure a safe and peaceful future for the world.

No provision was more dear to Wilson, and the Allied diplomats knew it. They ganged up on him and threatened to remove the 14th point if he did not make other concessions to their liking. One by one, Wilson sacrificed his principles for a just and lasting peace in order to save the League of Nations.

On June 28, 1919, the Treaty of Versailles was signed amid much pomp and pageantry. It was five years to the day after the assassination of Franz Ferdinand.

The terms of the treaty were harsh. Germany lost some of its territory, all of its colonies, its whole air force and most of its navy. The German army was to be permanently reduced to 100,000 men.

Most humiliating of all, the Germans were told they would have to pay for much of the cost of the war. Not only would Germany have to struggle to repair the damage to its own war-ravaged economy, it was also expected to compensate the Allies financially, right down to pensions for French soldiers. Economists predicted that it would take more than half a century for Germany to pay this debt, known as a war indemnity.

The German people were outraged. Citizens had begun to move toward democratic government, but the anger, fear and economic hardship caused by the treaty helped extremist groups gain power. Within a few years, right-wing militarist factions would again control the government. In this way, the Treaty of Versailles sowed the seeds of World War II.

President Wilson returned to the United States in July 1919. Except for one brief return, he had been overseas more than six months. The America he came back to was not the same nation he had led to war.

The public mood had changed. Most people no longer cared about the rest of the world. They wanted things to be the way they had been before the war. They were tired of "foreign entanglements" and favored America's return to isolation. Citizens began to rally under the slogan "Back to Normalcy."

Americans were feeling the stress of social changes that the war had caused. Before 1914, American industry's ever-growing hunger for cheap labor was fed by millions of immigrants, mainly from Europe. Then the war came and the valve was shut tight. The United States faced a labor shortage at the very moment its industry was about to boom. Where were new workers going to come from?

One source was the black man. Most blacks lived in the rural South. Most of America's industry was in the North. Labor agents for large companies combed through the South looking for black workers to do the unskilled jobs formerly done by foreign immigrants.

Lured by promises of higher wages and better treatment, hundreds of thousands of blacks moved to northern cities. Most settled in Detroit, Chicago, Pittsburgh, Philadelphia and New York. The sudden strain on these communities sometimes proved too much. Race riots broke out. In 1918, when American negro soldiers were fighting and dying on the Western Front, dozens of African-American citizens were being lynched in the states.

When American men started marching off to war, the economy turned to American women to take their place. Across the country women

WOMEN WORK THE ASSEMBLY LINES IN
INDUSTRIAL WAR EFFORT.
(NATIONAL ARCHIVES)

worked in the shipyards, the steel mills, the coal mines and on the farm, filling in for their absent husbands, fathers, brothers and sons.

Over four million men had served in the armed forces, half of them overseas. Released from the service, they wanted their jobs back. Women were expected to become docile housewives again.

American women had other ideas. They had helped win the war and felt that they should no longer be treated as second-class citizens. They formed political activist groups to demand the same privileges as men, including the right to vote. American women got this right in 1920.

Thus, the First World War released social forces in America from which there was no turning back. Faced with the dilemmas of social change, Americans lost interest in making the world safe for democracy.

A WOMAN BORING OUT A CANNON AT A
NEW ENGLAND ARSENAL.
(NATIONAL ARCHIVES)

During Wilson's long absence, his political opponents waged a persistent "Back to Normalcy" campaign on Capitol Hill. They ripped the president's peace plans to pieces. Wilson decided to take his message to the people. On September 3, 1919, still worn and tired from his nerve-racking trials at Versailles, he set off to make speeches across the nation. Wilson's journey took him 8,000 miles in 22 days, during which he made 37 addresses. Exhaustion finally overcame him. On September 26, Wilson suffered a stroke and was partially paralyzed.

Congress did not ratify the Treaty of Versailles. The United States would never join the League of Nations. So strong was the political pressure to return to isolationist policies that Congress even repealed the Declaration of War against the Central Powers.

Without the United States, the League of Nations, led by Britain and France, was hopelessly impotent. Germany rebuilt her war machine. In 1933 a new military dictator came to power. A former German army corporal who fought the doughboys in the Argonne, his name was Adolf Hitler.

Americans lived it up in the Roaring Twenties, then paid for it in the Depression of the Thirties, and then went back to fight the Germans in the Forties. Many historians believe that World War II was basically the second installment of the Great War of 1914–18.

Few people in 1919 could have imagined that the treaty that ended the "war to end war" would keep the peace for only two decades. Yet there were some who saw the storm clouds looming on the distant horizon. The Old Soldier, American General Tasker H. Bliss, who was at Versailles, wrote in his diary:

"We are in for a high period, followed by a low period. Then there will be the devil to pay all around the world."

BIBLIOGRAPHY

Burner, David; Marcus, Robert; Rosenberg, Emily. *America: A Portrait in History*. Prentice-Hall Inc., 1974.

De Kay, Ormond. *Imperialism and World War I*, New York: Golden Press, 1966.

Everette, Susan. *World War I*. Chicago: Rand McNally, 1980.

Ferrell, Robert. *Woodrow Wilson and World War I*. New York: Harper and Row, 1985.

Freidel, Frank. *Over There*. Boston: Little, Brown, 1964.

Gies, Joseph. *Crisis 1918*. New York: W.W. Norton, 1974.

Gurney, Gene. *Flying Aces of World War I*. New York: Scholastic Book Services, 1965.

Holden, Matthew. *War in the Trenches*. Hove, England: Wayland Publishers Ltd., 1973.

Josephy, Alvin M. (Editor-in-Charge). *World War I*. New York: American Heritage, 1964.

Morton, Frederic. *Thunder at Twilight*. New York: Scribners, 1989.

Robbins, Keith. *The First World War*. Oxford: Oxford University Press, 1984.

Simpson, Colin. *The Lusitania*. Boston: Little Brown, 1972.

Sulzberger, C.L. *The Fall of Eagles*. New York: Crown, 1977.

Suskind, Richard. *The Battle of Belleau Wood*, Toronto: Macmillan, 1969.

Tuchman, Barbara. *The Guns of August*. New York: Macmillan, 1962.

Welsh, Douglas. *The USA in World War I*. New York: Galahad Books, 1982.

Woodward, David. *Armies of the World, 1854–1914*. New York: Putnam, 1978.

INDEX